Winter

Homeschooling

JOURNAL

Name: ruth

Age: 8

Address:

Date: DEG16/2019/mon

INSTRUCTIONS

LIST EIGHT THINGS - That you want to learn about:

1. Iceland '
2. how was electricity created / discovered?'
3. how was PLANT made
4. moscow
5. how was paper made
6. how was the 1st steam engine computer made
7. kive l
8. inea l
   ireland

Action Steps:

1. Go to the library or bookstore.

2. Bring home a stack of at least eight interesting books and movies about these topics. Choose some books that have diagrams, instructions and illustrations.

Supplies Needed:

You will need pencils, colored pencils, pens and markers. If learning from YouTube you need internet and a viewing device.

Choose EIGHT Books To Use As School Books!

1. Write down the titles on each cover below.
2. Keep your stack of books in a safe place.
3. Be ready to read a few pages from your books daily.
4. Complete 5 or 6 pages each day in this workbook.

ICeLanP

moscow

kevi

inpa

how was The 1st vepo Game mape

how was The 1st paper mape

how was electricity mape orpiscovp

i reland

This page is for other books that you may use.

1. Write down the titles on each cover below.
2. Keep your stack of books in a safe place.
3. Be ready to read a few pages from your books daily.
4. Complete 5 or 6 pages each day in this workbook.

Circle
Today's Date

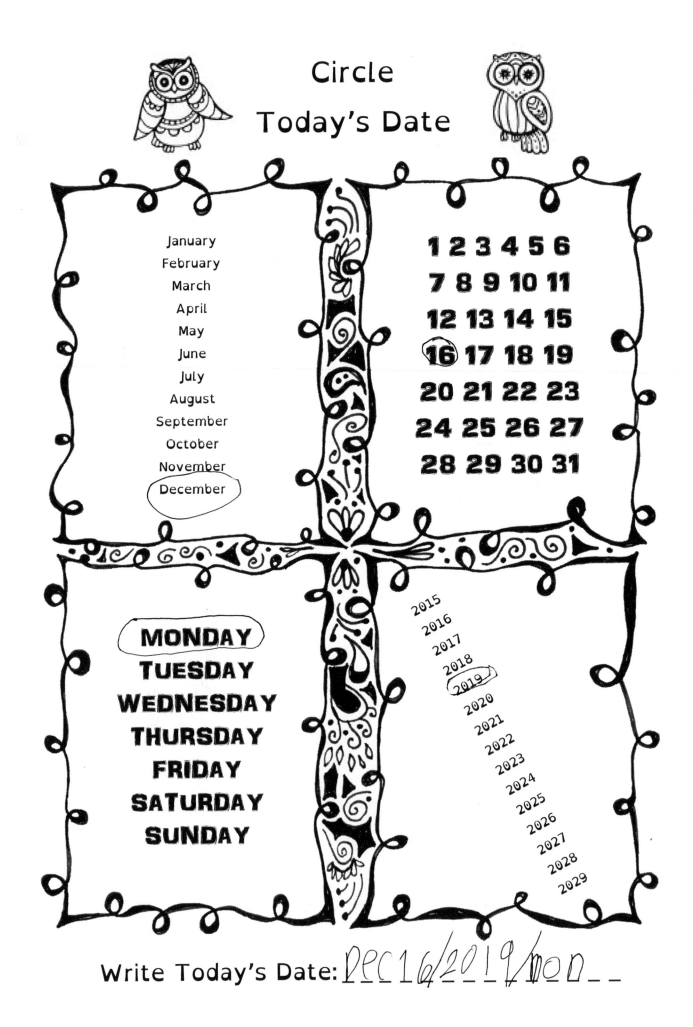

January
February
March
April
May
June
July
August
September
October
November
(December)

1 2 3 4 5 6
7 8 9 10 11
12 13 14 15
(16) 17 18 19
20 21 22 23
24 25 26 27
28 29 30 31

(MONDAY)
TUESDAY
WEDNESDAY
THURSDAY
FRIDAY
SATURDAY
SUNDAY

2015
2016
2017
2018
(2019)
2020
2021
2022
2023
2024
2025
2026
2027
2028
2029

Write Today's Date: DEC 16/2019/MON__

Nature Study

Go outside and make a realistic drawing of something you find in nature.

Draw a Meal
PLAN

Breakfast
Oats
milk

Lunch
nuts
BLUEBrrs

Dinner
Olives
Cron

Slaw
Birrs

Dessert

Reading Time - 1 Hour

Choose Four Books - Read from each book for 15 minutes.

Copy a sentence or picture from each book here:

Learning a Skill

Have a lesson, watch a tutorial or practice your skill.

I am learning how to:

DATE:

TIME:

Goals:

Notes:

Notes:

Circle
Today's Date

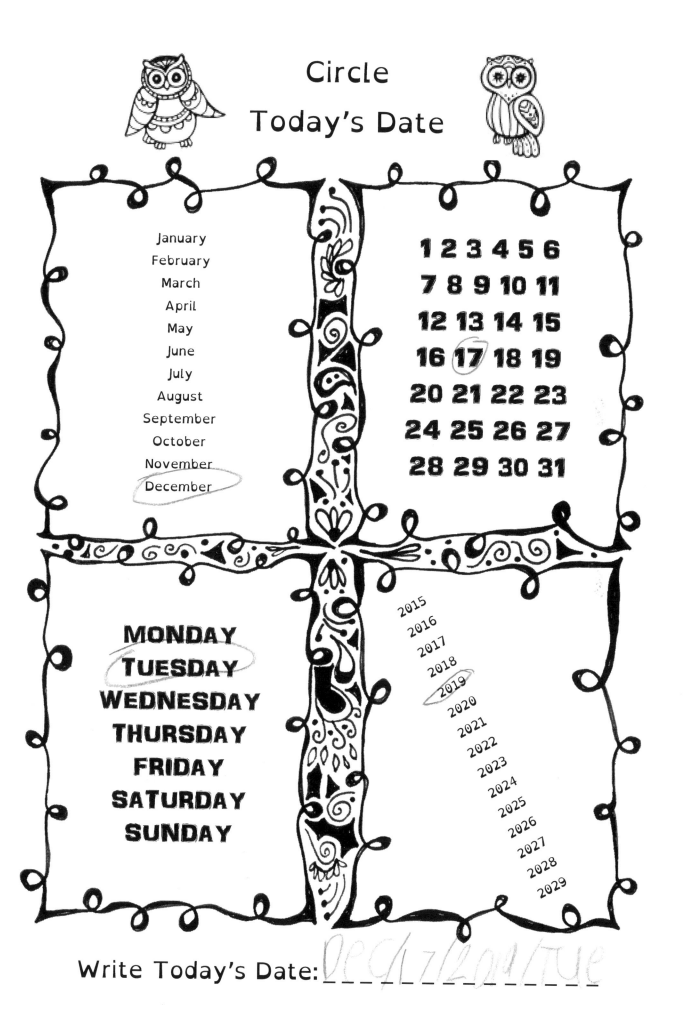

January
February
March
April
May
June
July
August
September
October
November
~~December~~

1 2 3 4 5 6
7 8 9 10 11
12 13 14 15
16 (17) 18 19
20 21 22 23
24 25 26 27
28 29 30 31

MONDAY
~~**TUESDAY**~~
WEDNESDAY
THURSDAY
FRIDAY
SATURDAY
SUNDAY

2015
2016
2017
2018
~~2019~~
2020
2021
2022
2023
2024
2025
2026
2027
2028
2029

Write Today's Date: DEC 17/2019/tue

My Illustrated TO-DO List

Spelling Time

Find 20 Words with **7** letters each.
Look in your books for words.
Write the words here:

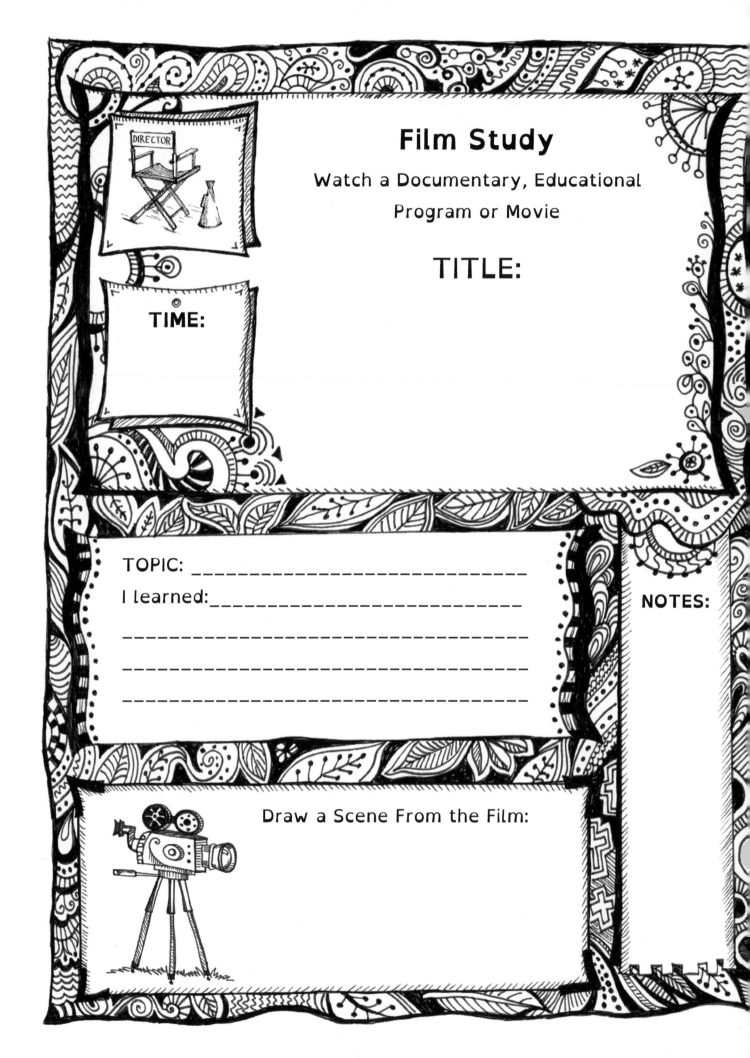

Film Study

Watch a Documentary, Educational Program or Movie

TITLE:

TIME:

TOPIC: _____

I learned: _____

_____

_____

_____

NOTES:

Draw a Scene From the Film:

Copywork

Find an interesting paragraph in one of your books and copy it. Be diligent to make your writing look exactly like it does in the book.

TITLE:_____ **Page Number:_____**

_____

_____

_____

_____

_____

_____

_____

_____

_____

_____

_____

_____

_____

_____

Write & Draw
about something that
really happened.

_____

_____

_____

_____

_____

_____

_____

_____

_____

_____

Circle
Today's Date

January
February
March
April
May
June
July
August
September
October
November
December

1 2 3 4 5 6
7 8 9 10 11
12 13 14 15
16 17 18 19
20 21 22 23
24 25 26 27
28 29 30 31

MONDAY
TUESDAY
WEDNESDAY
THURSDAY
FRIDAY
SATURDAY
SUNDAY

2015
2016
2017
2018
2019
2020
2021
2022
2023
2024
2025
2026
2027
2028
2029

Write Today's Date: _____

My Thinking Page

This is where you write down your ideas, goals,
and plans - with a thankful heart!

Ideas

Goals

7

I Am Thankful For...

Checklist

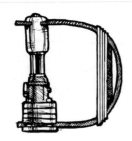

Design Something

Use this graph paper to design something.
If you can't think of anything design a house.

Film Study

Watch a Documentary, Educational Program or Movie

TITLE:

TIME:

TOPIC: _____

I learned: _____

_____

_____

_____

NOTES:

Draw a Scene From the Film:

Art & Creativity Time

Reading Time - 1 Hour

Choose Four Books - Read from each book for 15 minutes.

Copy a sentence or picture from each book here:

Circle
Today's Date

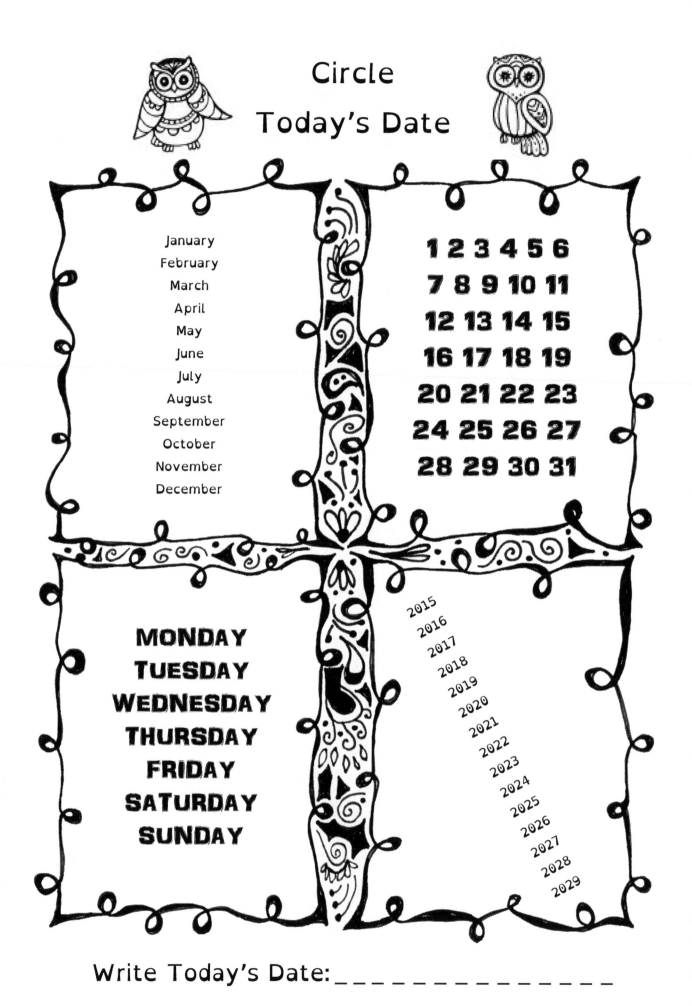

January
February
March
April
May
June
July
August
September
October
November
December

1 2 3 4 5 6
7 8 9 10 11
12 13 14 15
16 17 18 19
20 21 22 23
24 25 26 27
28 29 30 31

MONDAY
TUESDAY
WEDNESDAY
THURSDAY
FRIDAY
SATURDAY
SUNDAY

2015
2016
2017
2018
2019
2020
2021
2022
2023
2024
2025
2026
2027
2028
2029

Write Today's Date: _ _ _ _ _ _ _ _ _ _ _ _ _ _ _ _

My Thinking Page

This is where you write down your ideas, goals, and plans - with a thankful heart!

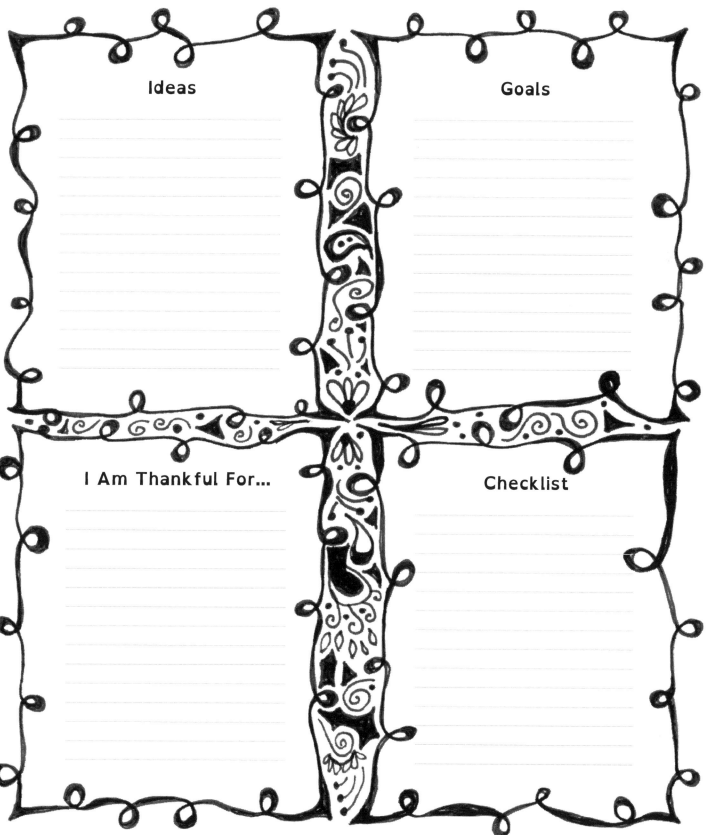

Ideas

Goals

I Am Thankful For...

Checklist

Nature Study

Go outside and make a realistic drawing of something you find in nature.

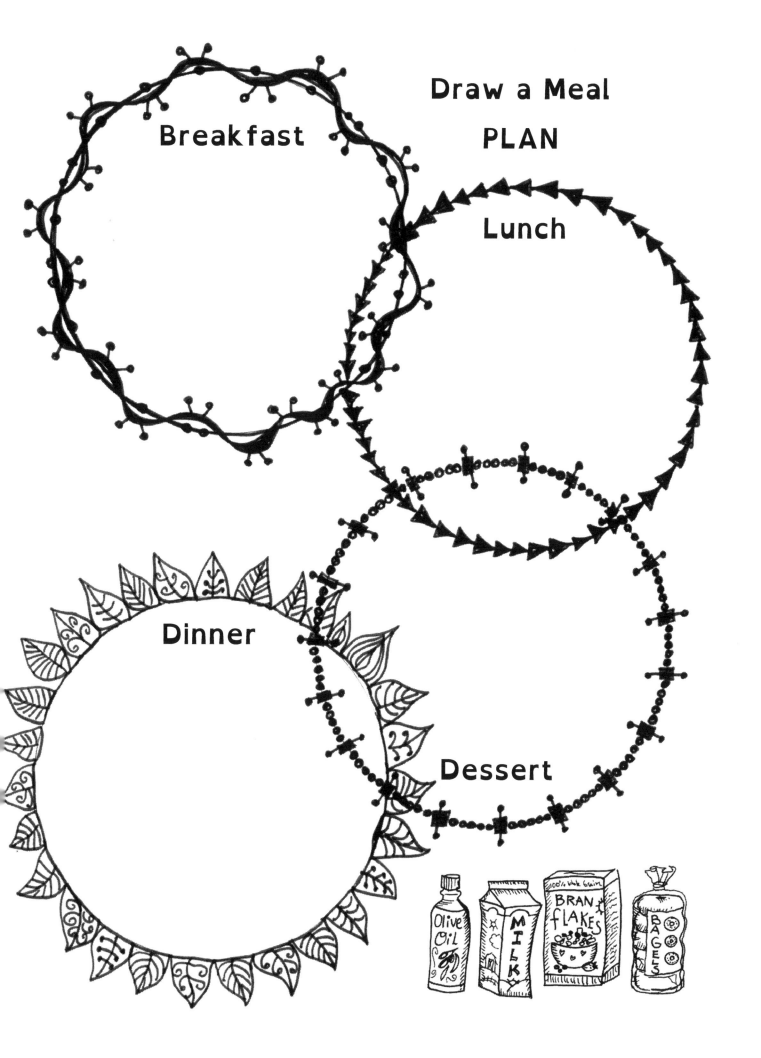

Draw a Meal
PLAN

Breakfast

Lunch

Dinner

Dessert

Recipe:

_____

Serves:

Prep Time:

Ingredients:

Instructions:

Shopping List:

Open a cookbook, learn from mom or look online for
some wonderful recipes!

Reading Time - 1 Hour

Choose Four Books - Read from each book for 15 minutes.

Copy a sentence or picture from each book here:

Write & Draw
about something that
really happened.

_____
_____
_____
_____
_____
_____
_____
_____
_____
_____

Circle
Today's Date

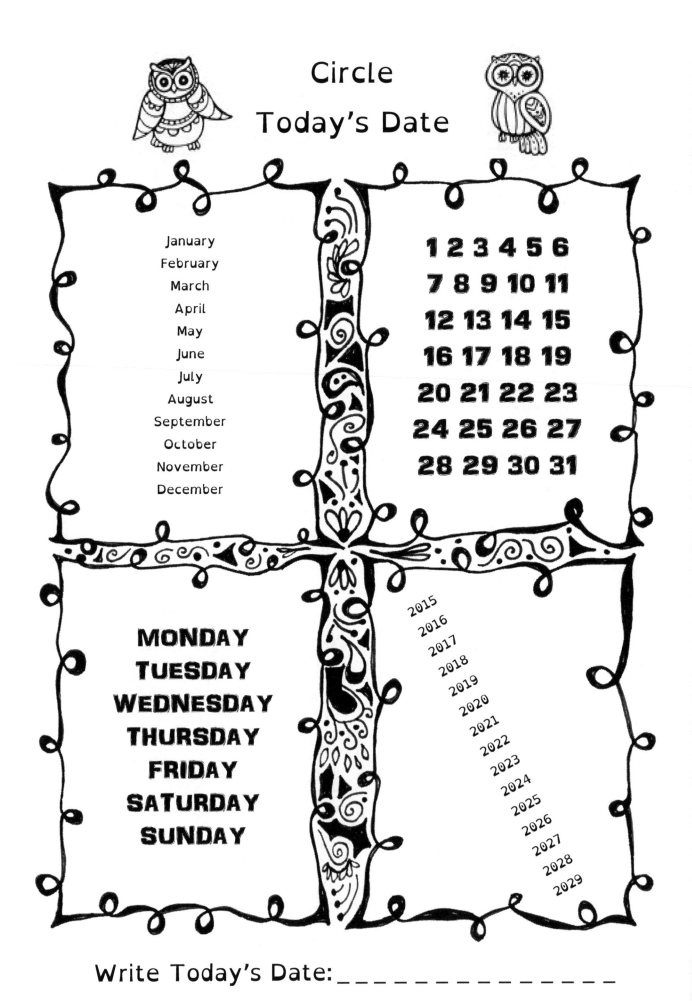

January
February
March
April
May
June
July
August
September
October
November
December

1 2 3 4 5 6
7 8 9 10 11
12 13 14 15
16 17 18 19
20 21 22 23
24 25 26 27
28 29 30 31

MONDAY
TUESDAY
WEDNESDAY
THURSDAY
FRIDAY
SATURDAY
SUNDAY

2015
2016
2017
2018
2019
2020
2021
2022
2023
2024
2025
2026
2027
2028
2029

Write Today's Date: _ _ _ _ _ _ _ _ _ _ _ _ _ _ _

My Illustrated TO-DO List

Spelling Time

Find 20 Words with 5 letters each.
Look in your books for words.
Write the words here:

Learning a Skill

Have a lesson, watch a tutorial or practice your skill.

I am learning how to:

DATE:

TIME:

Goals:

Notes:

Notes:

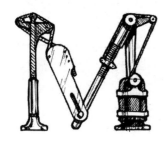

Math Practice

Watch a math tutorial or open up a math book.

You can practice math problems here.

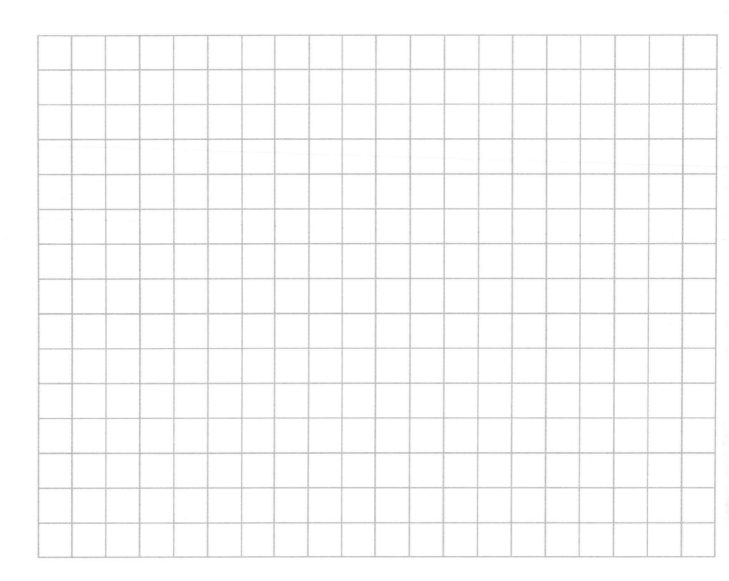

Copywork

Find an interesting paragraph in one of your books and copy it. Be diligent to make your writing look exactly like it does in the book.

TITLE:_____ **Page Number:**_____

_____

_____

_____

_____

_____

_____

_____

_____

_____

_____

_____

_____

_____

_____

_____

Sketch a Picture

Look through your library books and find something to draw.

Circle Today's Date

January
February
March
April
May
June
July
August
September
October
November
December

1 2 3 4 5 6
7 8 9 10 11
12 13 14 15
16 17 18 19
20 21 22 23
24 25 26 27
28 29 30 31

MONDAY
TUESDAY
WEDNESDAY
THURSDAY
FRIDAY
SATURDAY
SUNDAY

2015
2016
2017
2018
2019
2020
2021
2022
2023
2024
2025
2026
2027
2028
2029

Write Today's Date: _ _ _ _ _ _ _ _ _ _ _ _ _ _ _ _ _

Nature Study

Go outside and make a realistic drawing of something you find in nature.

My Thinking Page

This is where you write down your ideas, goals, and plans - with a thankful heart!

Ideas

Goals

I Am Thankful For...

Checklist

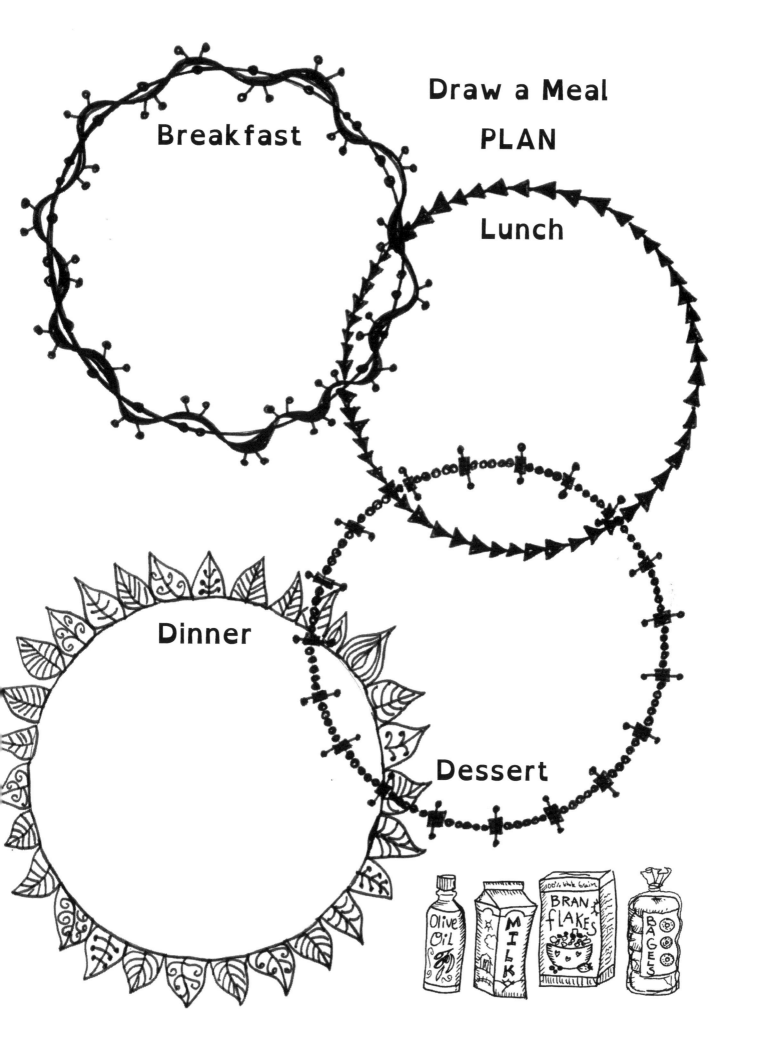

Breakfast

Draw a Meal
PLAN

Lunch

Dinner

Dessert

Recipe:

Serves:

Prep Time:

Ingredients:

Instructions:

Shopping List:

Open a cookbook, learn from mom or look online for
some wonderful recipes!

Creative Writing

Draw a picture below.

Write a poem or short story about it.

TITLE: _____

_____
_____
_____
_____
_____
_____
_____
_____
_____
_____
_____
_____
_____

Reading Time - 1 Hour

Choose Four Books - Read from each book for 15 minutes.

Copy a sentence or picture from each book here:

Circle Today's Date

January	**1 2 3 4 5 6**
February	**7 8 9 10 11**
March	**12 13 14 15**
April	**16 17 18 19**
May	**20 21 22 23**
June	**24 25 26 27**
July	**28 29 30 31**
August	
September	
October	
November	
December	

MONDAY
TUESDAY
WEDNESDAY
THURSDAY
FRIDAY
SATURDAY
SUNDAY

2015
2016
2017
2018
2019
2020
2021
2022
2023
2024
2025
2026
2027
2028
2029

Write Today's Date: _ _ _ _ _ _ _ _ _ _ _ _ _ _ _

My Illustrated TO-DO List

Spelling Time

Find 20 Words with 6 letters each.
Look in your books for words.
Write the words here:

_____   _____

_____   _____

_____   _____

_____   _____

_____   _____

_____   _____

_____   _____

_____   _____

_____   _____

_____   _____

Film Study

Watch a Documentary, Educational Program or Movie

TITLE:

TIME:

TOPIC: _____

I learned:_____

_____

_____

_____

NOTES:

Draw a Scene From the Film:

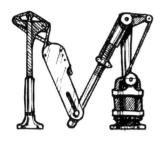

Math Practice

Watch a math tutorial or open up a math book.

You can practice math problems here.

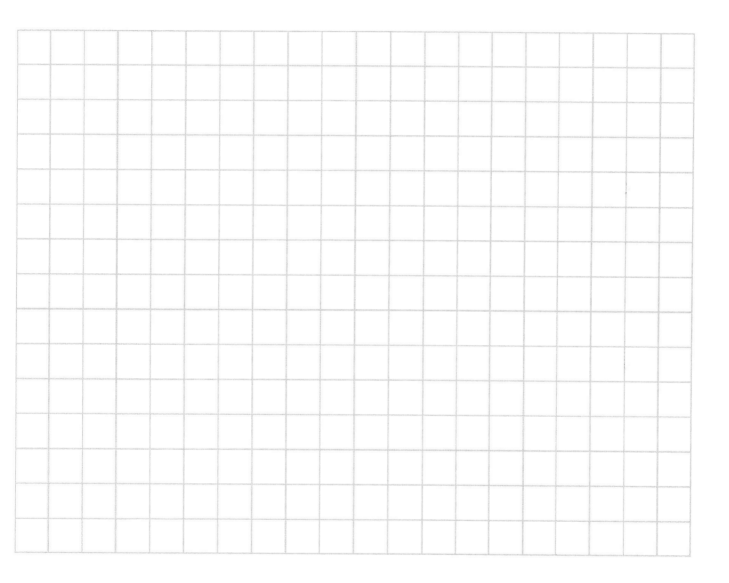

Copywork

Find an interesting paragraph in one of your books and copy it. Be diligent to make your writing look exactly like it does in the book.

TITLE:_____ **Page Number:**_____

_____

_____

_____

_____

_____

_____

_____

_____

_____

_____

_____

_____

_____

_____

Sketch a Picture

Look through your library books and find something to draw.

Circle
Today's Date

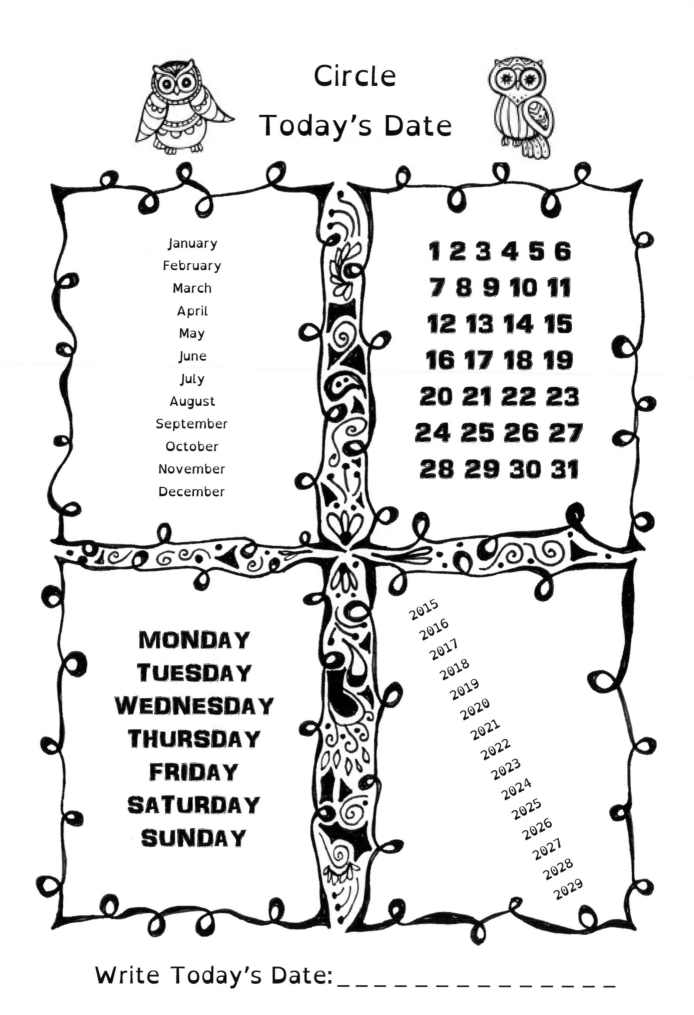

January
February
March
April
May
June
July
August
September
October
November
December

1 2 3 4 5 6
7 8 9 10 11
12 13 14 15
16 17 18 19
20 21 22 23
24 25 26 27
28 29 30 31

MONDAY
TUESDAY
WEDNESDAY
THURSDAY
FRIDAY
SATURDAY
SUNDAY

2015
2016
2017
2018
2019
2020
2021
2022
2023
2024
2025
2026
2027
2028
2029

Write Today's Date:_ _ _ _ _ _ _ _ _ _ _ _ _ _ _ _ _

My Thinking Page

This is where you write down your ideas, goals,
and plans - with a thankful heart!

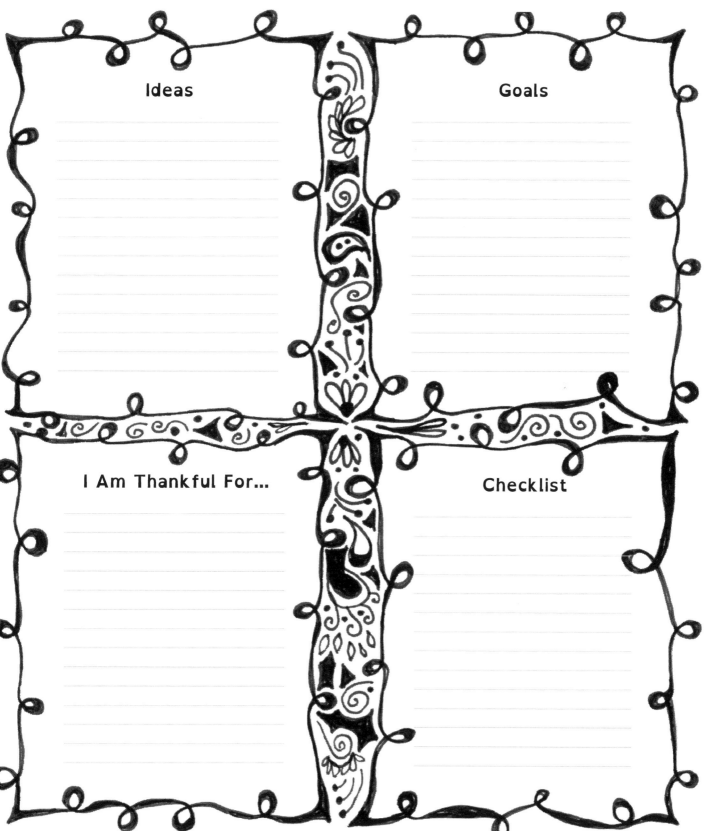

Ideas

Goals

I Am Thankful For...

Checklist

Nature Study

Go outside and make a realistic
drawing of something you find in nature.

Creative Writing

Draw a picture below.

Write a poem or short story about it.

TITLE: _____

_____
_____
_____
_____
_____
_____
_____
_____
_____
_____
_____
_____
_____

Reading Time - 1 Hour

Choose Four Books - Read from each book for 15 minutes.

Copy a sentence or picture from each book here:

Listening Time

Listen to an audio book or classical music or
ask someone to read a story to you while
you color and draw on the next page.

What are you listening to?

_____

Circle
Today's Date

January
February
March
April
May
June
July
August
September
October
November
December

1 2 3 4 5 6
7 8 9 10 11
12 13 14 15
16 17 18 19
20 21 22 23
24 25 26 27
28 29 30 31

MONDAY
TUESDAY
WEDNESDAY
THURSDAY
FRIDAY
SATURDAY
SUNDAY

2015
2016
2017
2018
2019
2020
2021
2022
2023
2024
2025
2026
2027
2028
2029

Write Today's Date: _____

My Thinking Page

This is where you write down your ideas, goals, and plans - with a thankful heart!

Ideas

Goals

I Am Thankful For...

Checklist

Art & Creativity Time

Spelling Time

Find 20 Words with 7 letters each.

Look in your books for words.

Write the words here:

Learning a Skill

Have a lesson, watch a tutorial or practice your skill.

I am learning how to:

DATE:

TIME:

Goals:

Notes:

Notes:

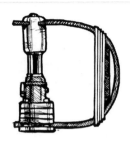

Design Something

Use this graph paper to design something.

If you can't think of anything design a house.

Copywork

Find an interesting paragraph in one of your books and copy it. Be diligent to make your writing look exactly like it does in the book.

TITLE:_____ **Page Number:**_____

_____

_____

_____

_____

_____

_____

_____

_____

_____

_____

_____

_____

_____

_____

Sketch a Picture

Look through your library books and find something to draw.

Circle
Today's Date

January
February
March
April
May
June
July
August
September
October
November
December

1 2 3 4 5 6
7 8 9 10 11
12 13 14 15
16 17 18 19
20 21 22 23
24 25 26 27
28 29 30 31

MONDAY
TUESDAY
WEDNESDAY
THURSDAY
FRIDAY
SATURDAY
SUNDAY

2015
2016
2017
2018
2019
2020
2021
2022
2023
2024
2025
2026
2027
2028
2029

Write Today's Date: _ _ _ _ _ _ _ _ _ _ _ _ _ _ _ _

Nature Study

Go outside and make a realistic drawing of something you find in nature.

My Illustrated TO-DO List

Reading Time - 1 Hour

Choose Four Books - Read from each book for 15 minutes.

Copy a sentence or picture from each book here:

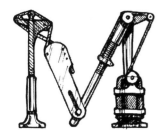

Math Practice

Watch a math tutorial or open up a math book.

You can practice math problems here.

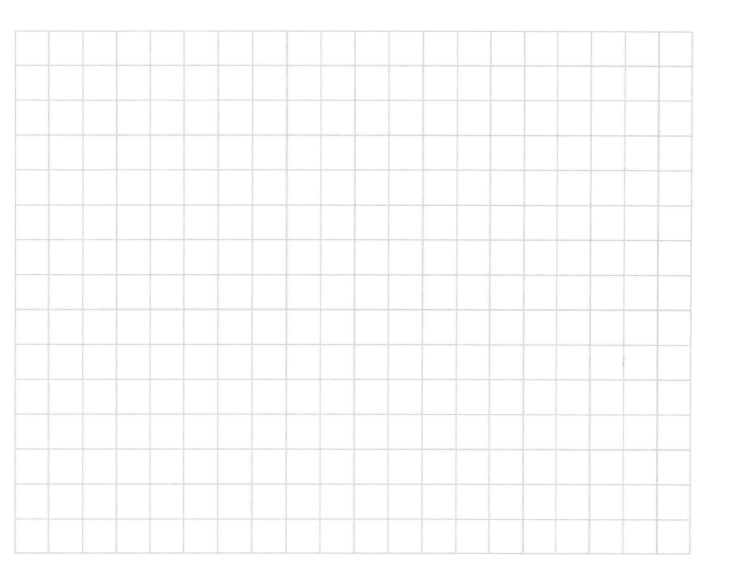

Write & Draw
about something that
really happened.

_____
_____
_____
_____
_____
_____
_____
_____
_____
_____

Circle
Today's Date

January
February
March
April
May
June
July
August
September
October
November
December

1 2 3 4 5 6
7 8 9 10 11
12 13 14 15
16 17 18 19
20 21 22 23
24 25 26 27
28 29 30 31

MONDAY
TUESDAY
WEDNESDAY
THURSDAY
FRIDAY
SATURDAY
SUNDAY

2015
2016
2017
2018
2019
2020
2021
2022
2023
2024
2025
2026
2027
2028
2029

Write Today's Date: _ _ _ _ _ _ _ _ _ _ _ _ _ _ _ _

My Illustrated TO-DO List

Listening Time

Listen to an audio book or classical music or
ask someone to read a story to you while
you color and draw on the next page.

What are you listening to?

_____

Spelling Time

Find 20 Words with **8** letters each.
Look in your books for words.
Write the words here:

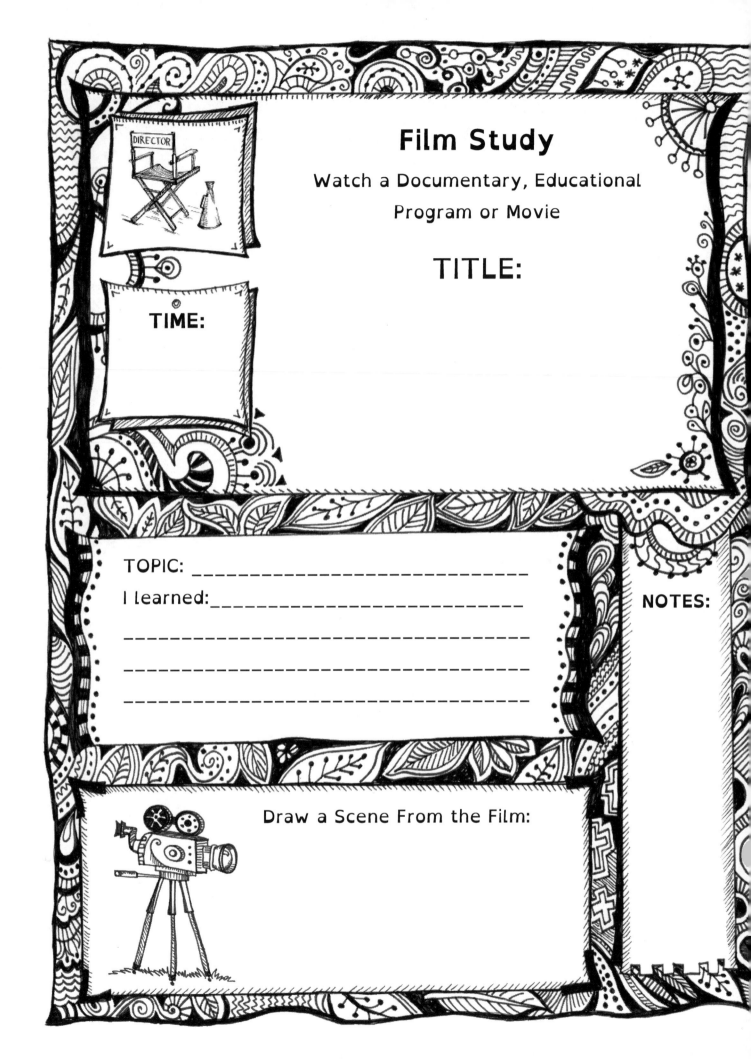

Film Study

Watch a Documentary, Educational Program or Movie

TITLE:

DIRECTOR

TIME:

TOPIC: _____

I learned:_____

_____

_____

_____

NOTES:

Draw a Scene From the Film:

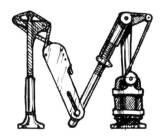

Math Practice

Watch a math tutorial or open up a math book.

You can practice math problems here.

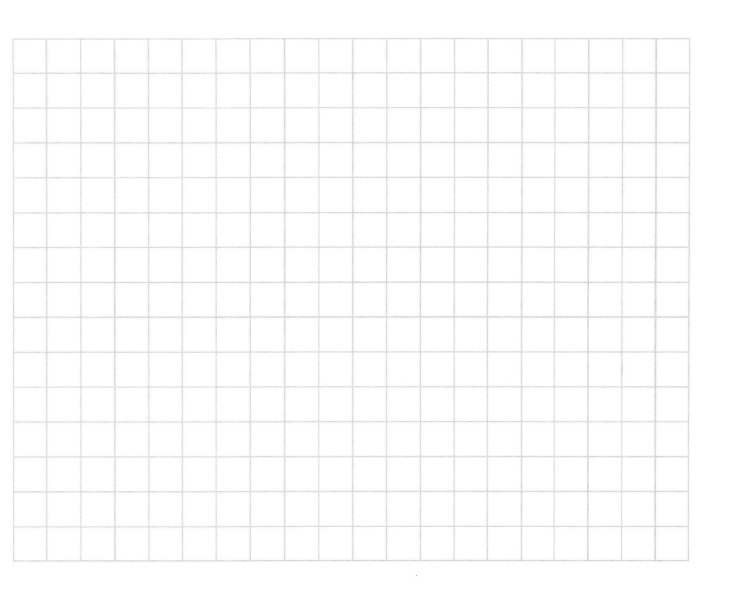

Sketch a Picture

Look through your library books and find something to draw.

Circle Today's Date

January
February
March
April
May
June
July
August
September
October
November
December

1 2 3 4 5 6
7 8 9 10 11
12 13 14 15
16 17 18 19
20 21 22 23
24 25 26 27
28 29 30 31

MONDAY
TUESDAY
WEDNESDAY
THURSDAY
FRIDAY
SATURDAY
SUNDAY

2015
2016
2017
2018
2019
2020
2021
2022
2023
2024
2025
2026
2027
2028
2029

Write Today's Date: _____

My Thinking Page

This is where you write down your ideas, goals,
and plans - with a thankful heart!

Ideas

Goals

I Am Thankful For...

Checklist

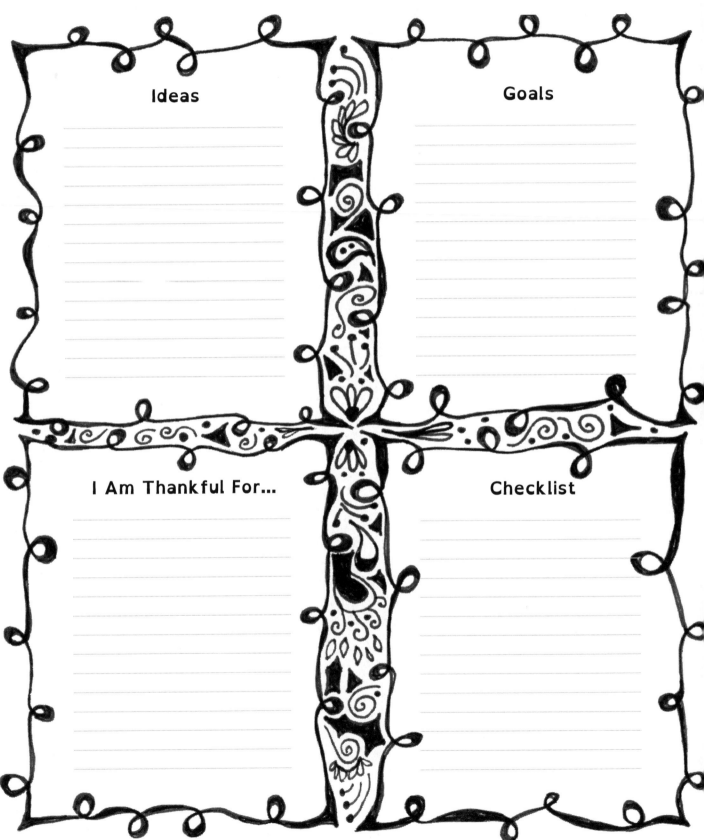

Nature Study

Go outside and make a realistic
drawing of something you find in nature.

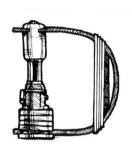

Design Something

Use this graph paper to design something.

If you can't think of anything design a house.

Write & Draw
about something that
really happened.

Reading Time - 1 Hour

Choose Four Books - Read from each book for 15 minutes.

Copy a sentence or picture from each book here:

Circle
Today's Date

January
February
March
April
May
June
July
August
September
October
November
December

1 2 3 4 5 6
7 8 9 10 11
12 13 14 15
16 17 18 19
20 21 22 23
24 25 26 27
28 29 30 31

MONDAY
TUESDAY
WEDNESDAY
THURSDAY
FRIDAY
SATURDAY
SUNDAY

2015
2016
2017
2018
2019
2020
2021
2022
2023
2024
2025
2026
2027
2028
2029

Write Today's Date:_____

My Thinking Page

This is where you write down your ideas, goals, and plans - with a thankful heart!

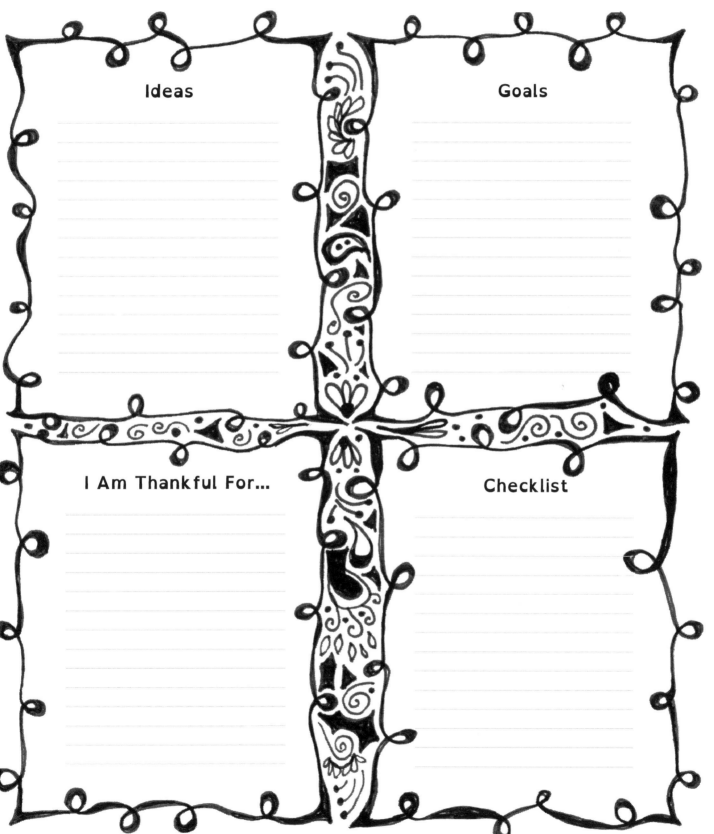

Ideas

Goals

I Am Thankful For...

Checklist

Art & Creativity Time

Learning a Skill

Have a lesson, watch a tutorial or practice your skill.

I am learning how to:

DATE:

TIME:

Goals:

Notes:

Notes:

Design Something

Use this graph paper to design something.

If you can't think of anything design a house.

Copywork

Find an interesting paragraph in one of your books and copy it. Be diligent to make your writing look exactly like it does in the book.

TITLE:_____ **Page Number:_____**

_____

_____

_____

_____

_____

_____

_____

_____

_____

_____

_____

_____

_____

_____

Circle
Today's Date

January
February
March
April
May
June
July
August
September
October
November
December

1 2 3 4 5 6
7 8 9 10 11
12 13 14 15
16 17 18 19
20 21 22 23
24 25 26 27
28 29 30 31

MONDAY
TUESDAY
WEDNESDAY
THURSDAY
FRIDAY
SATURDAY
SUNDAY

2015
2016
2017
2018
2019
2020
2021
2022
2023
2024
2025
2026
2027
2028
2029

Write Today's Date:_____

My Thinking Page

This is where you write down your ideas, goals,
and plans - with a thankful heart!

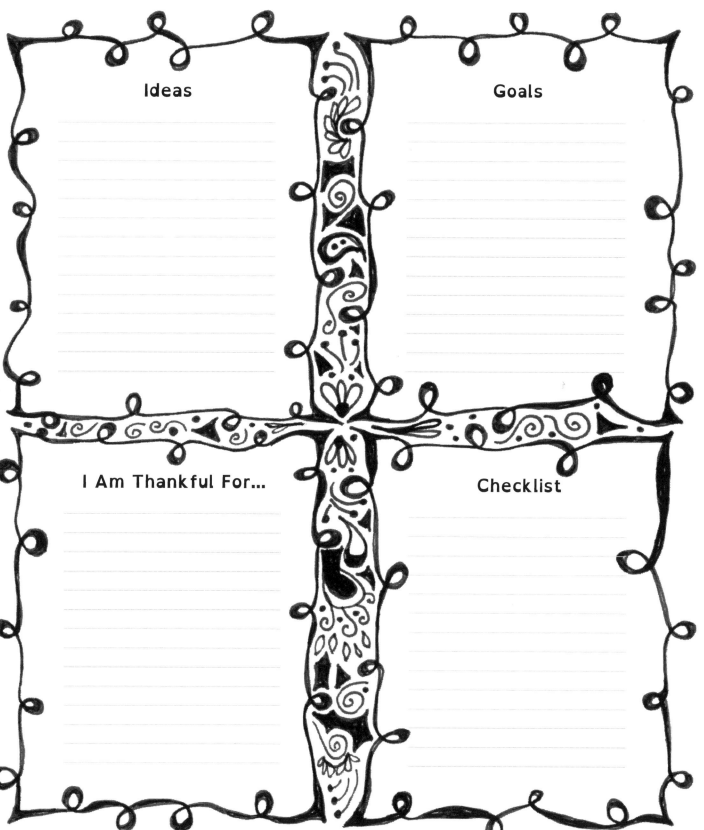

Ideas

Goals

I Am Thankful For...

Checklist

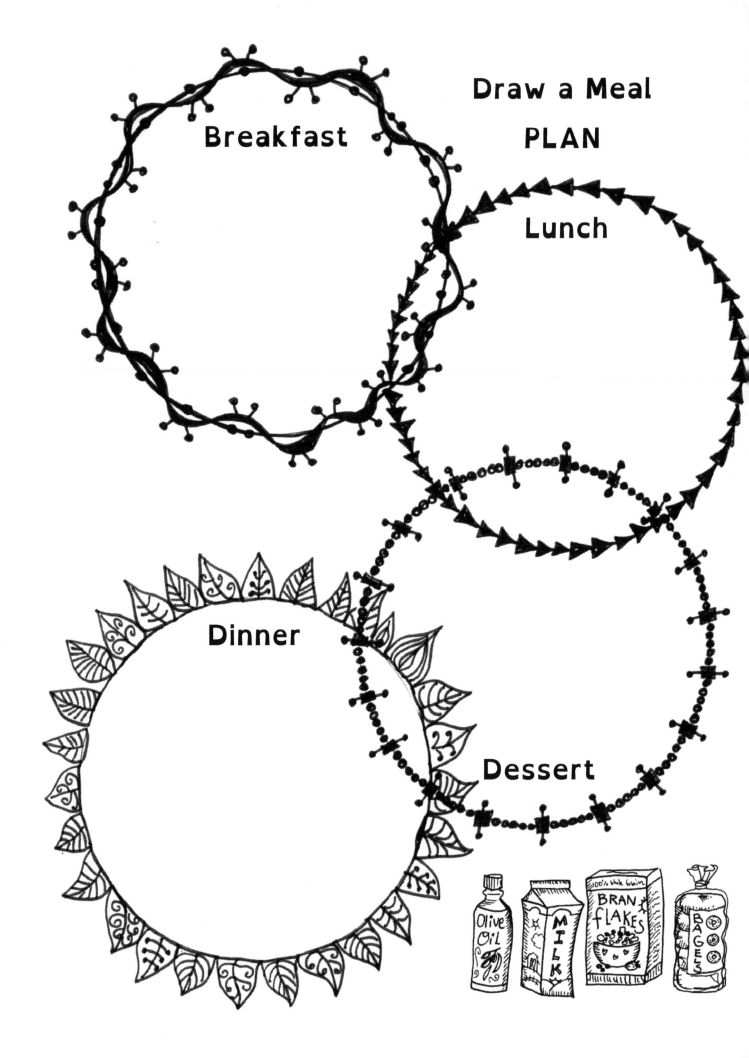

Draw a Meal
PLAN

Breakfast

Lunch

Dinner

Dessert

Recipe:

_____

Serves:

Prep Time:

Ingredients:

Instructions:

Shopping List:

Open a cookbook, learn from mom or look online for some wonderful recipes!

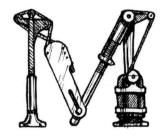

Math Practice

Watch a math tutorial or open up a math book.
You can practice math problems here.

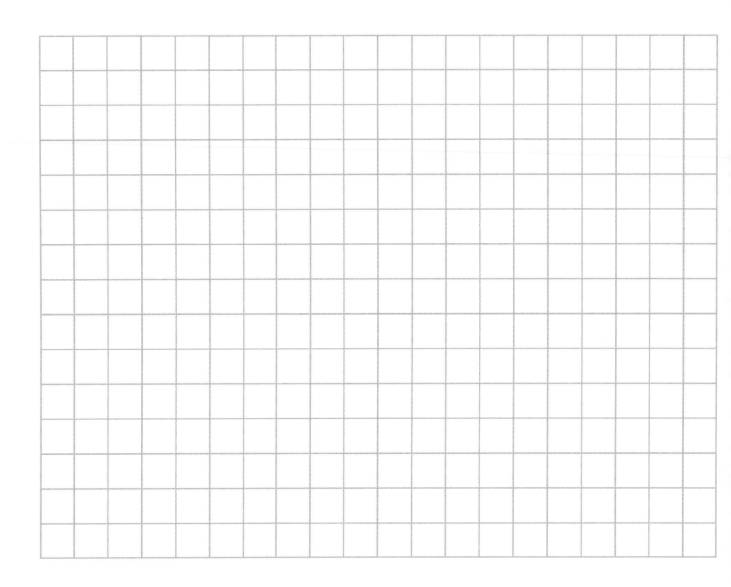

Write & Draw
about something that
really happened.

_____

_____

_____

_____

_____

_____

_____

_____

_____

Reading Time - 1 Hour

Choose Four Books - Read from each book for 15 minutes.

Copy a sentence or picture from each book here:

Circle
Today's Date

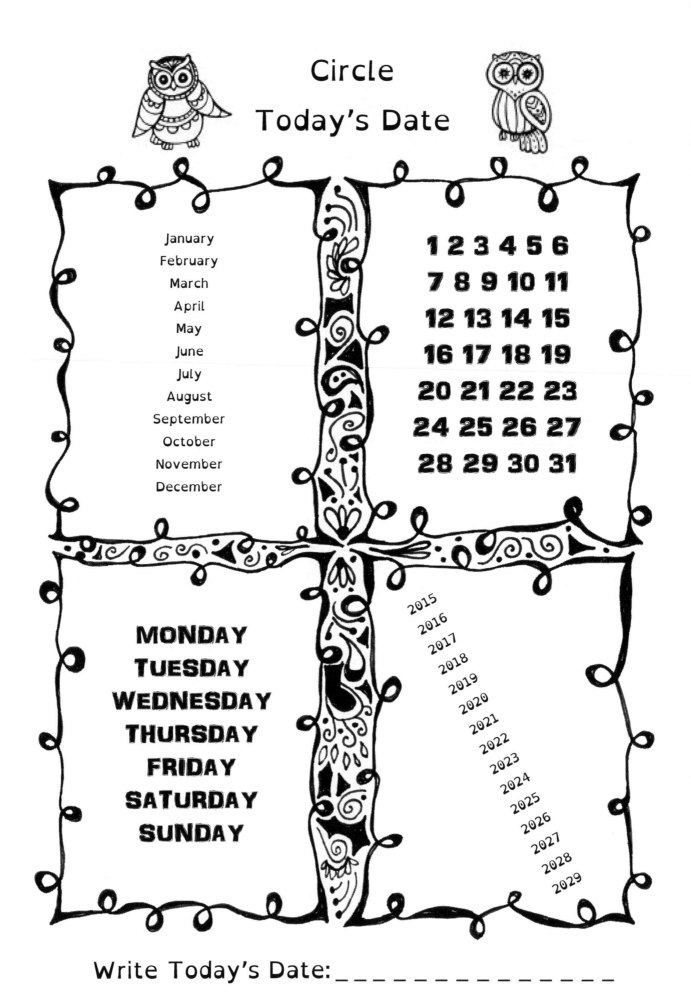

January	1 2 3 4 5 6
February	7 8 9 10 11
March	12 13 14 15
April	16 17 18 19
May	20 21 22 23
June	24 25 26 27
July	28 29 30 31
August	
September	
October	
November	
December	

MONDAY	2015
TUESDAY	2016
WEDNESDAY	2017
THURSDAY	2018
FRIDAY	2019
SATURDAY	2020
SUNDAY	2021
	2022
	2023
	2024
	2025
	2026
	2027
	2028
	2029

Write Today's Date: _____

My Illustrated TO-DO List

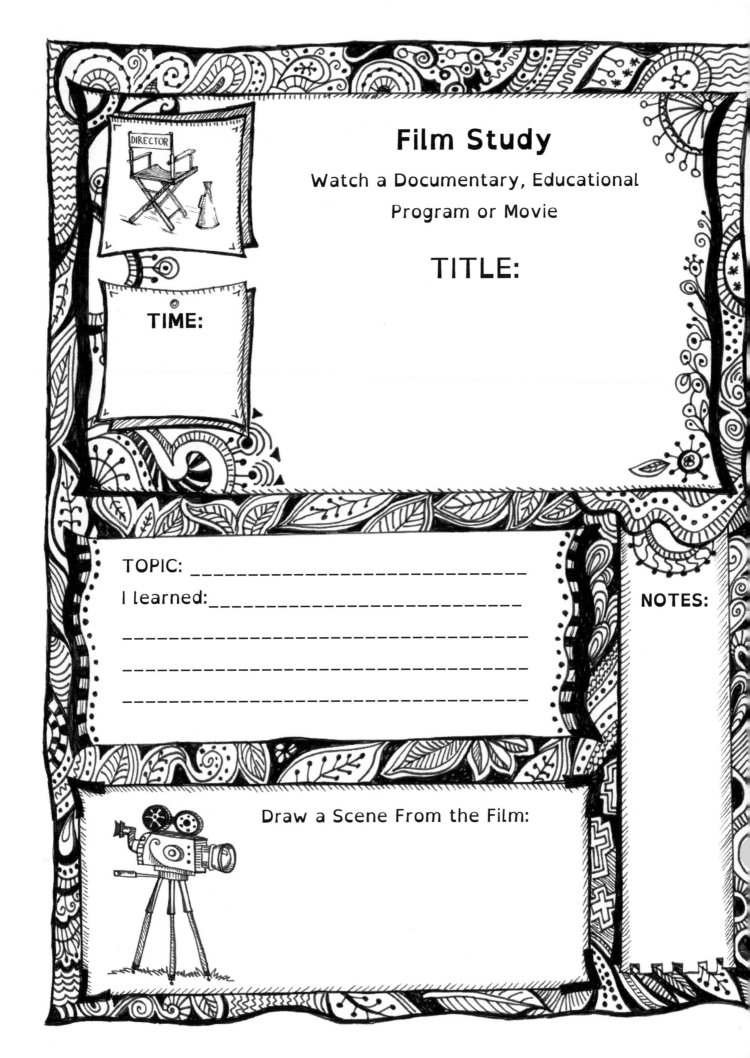

Film Study

Watch a Documentary, Educational Program or Movie

TITLE:

TIME:

TOPIC: _____

I learned: _____

_____

_____

_____

NOTES:

Draw a Scene From the Film:

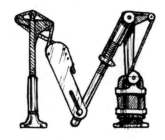

Math Practice

Watch a math tutorial or open up a math book.
You can practice math problems here.

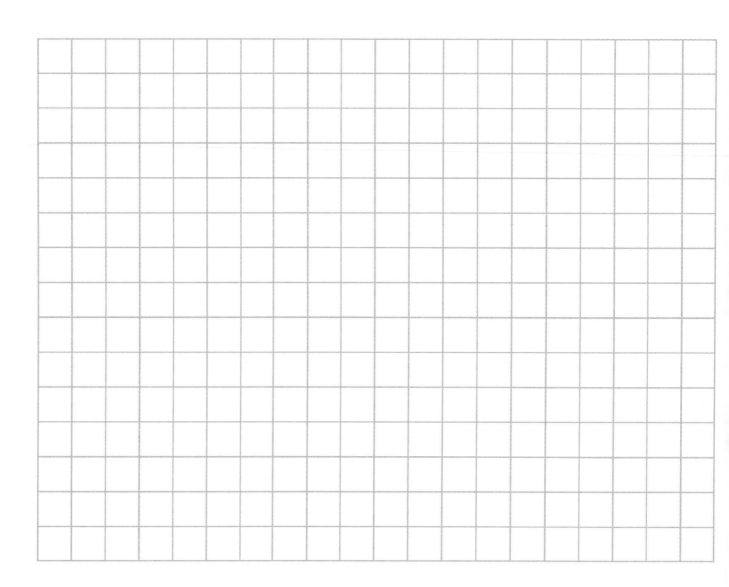

Copywork

Find an interesting paragraph in one of your books and copy it. Be diligent to make your writing look exactly like it does in the book.

TITLE:_____ **Page Number:_____**

_____

_____

_____

_____

_____

_____

_____

_____

_____

_____

_____

_____

_____

_____

Sketch a Picture

Look through your library books and find something to draw.

Circle
Today's Date

January
February
March
April
May
June
July
August
September
October
November
December

1 2 3 4 5 6
7 8 9 10 11
12 13 14 15
16 17 18 19
20 21 22 23
24 25 26 27
28 29 30 31

MONDAY
TUESDAY
WEDNESDAY
THURSDAY
FRIDAY
SATURDAY
SUNDAY

2015
2016
2017
2018
2019
2020
2021
2022
2023
2024
2025
2026
2027
2028
2029

Write Today's Date: _ _ _ _ _ _ _ _ _ _ _ _ _ _ _ _ _

My Thinking Page

This is where you write down your ideas, goals, and plans - with a thankful heart!

Ideas

Goals

I Am Thankful For...

Checklist

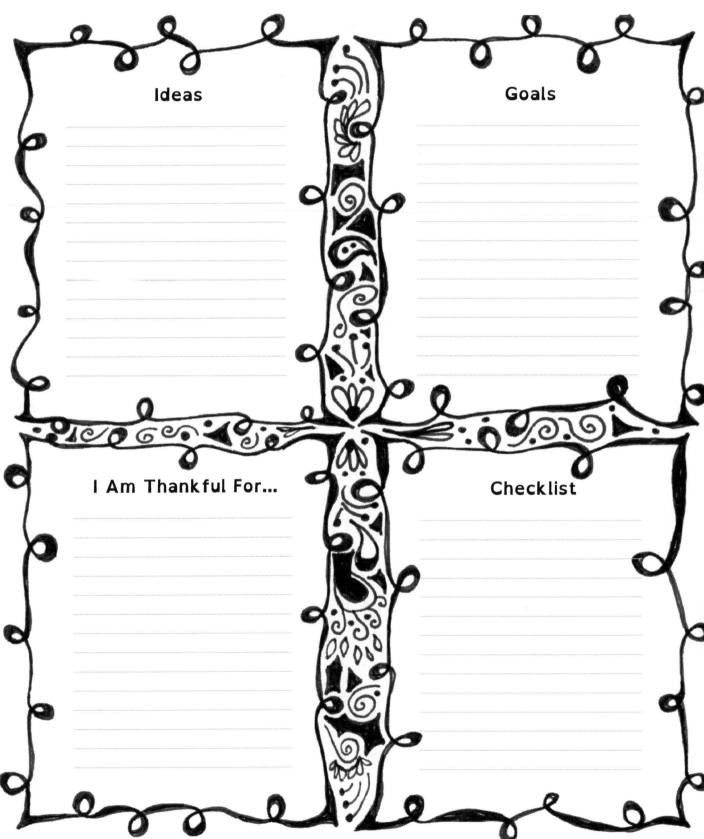

Nature Study

Go outside and make a realistic drawing of something you find in nature.

Creative Writing

Draw a picture below.

Write a poem or short story about it.

TITLE: _____

_____

_____

_____

_____

_____

_____

_____

_____

_____

_____

_____

_____

_____

Write & Draw
about something that
really happened.

_____

_____

_____

_____

_____

_____

_____

_____

_____

_____

Reading Time - 1 Hour

Choose Four Books - Read from each book for 15 minutes.

Copy a sentence or picture from each book here:

Circle
Today's Date

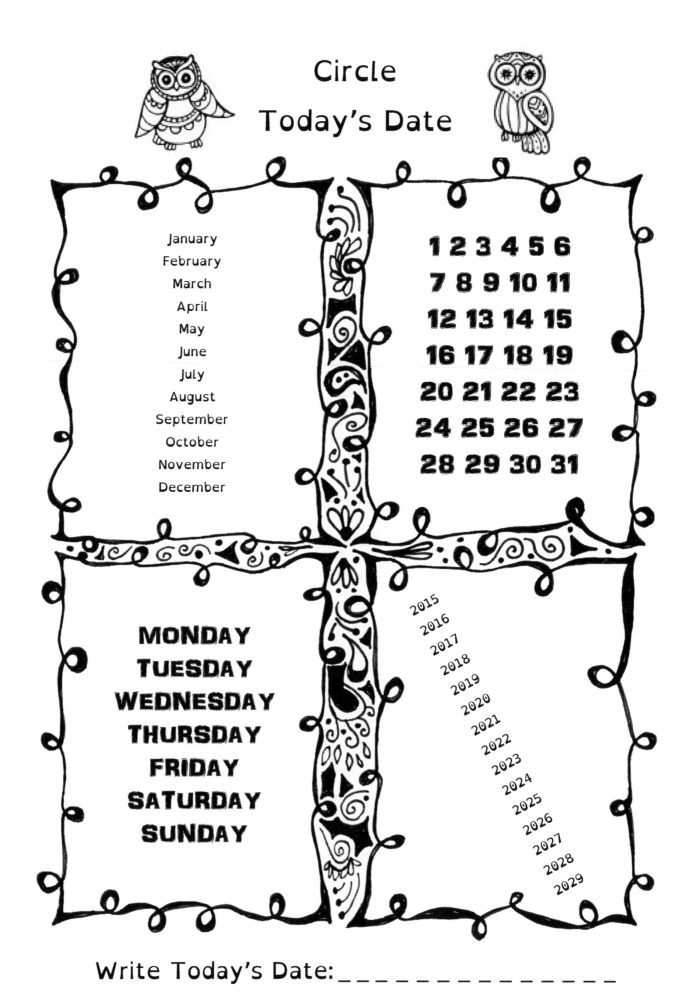

January
February
March
April
May
June
July
August
September
October
November
December

1 2 3 4 5 6
7 8 9 10 11
12 13 14 15
16 17 18 19
20 21 22 23
24 25 26 27
28 29 30 31

MONDAY
TUESDAY
WEDNESDAY
THURSDAY
FRIDAY
SATURDAY
SUNDAY

2015
2016
2017
2018
2019
2020
2021
2022
2023
2024
2025
2026
2027
2028
2029

Write Today's Date: _ _ _ _ _ _ _ _ _ _ _ _ _ _ _ _

Art & Creativity Time

Creative Writing

Draw a picture below.

Write a poem or short story about it.

TITLE: _____

_____
_____
_____
_____
_____
_____
_____
_____
_____
_____
_____
_____
_____
_____

Spelling Time

Find 20 Words with 7 letters each.
Look in your books for words.
Write the words here:

Film Study

Watch a Documentary, Educational Program or Movie

TITLE:

TIME:

TOPIC: _____

I learned: _____

_____

_____

_____

NOTES:

Draw a Scene From the Film:

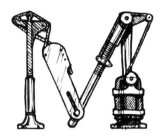

Math Practice

Watch a math tutorial or open up a math book.

You can practice math problems here.

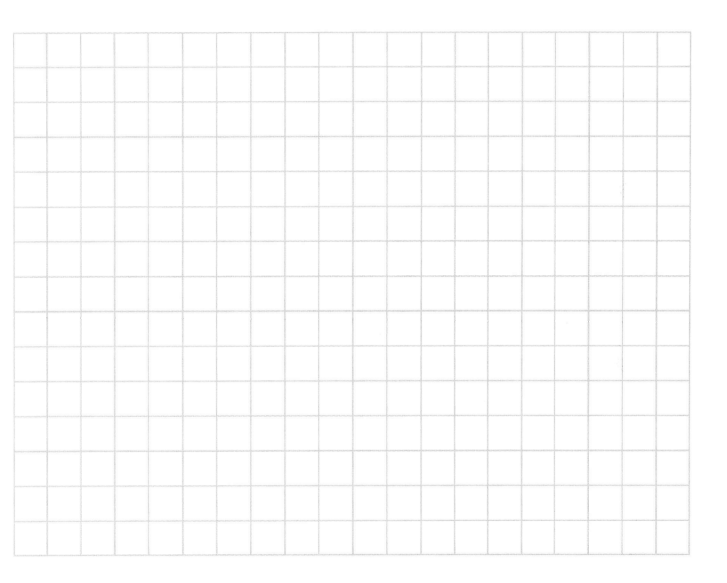

Copywork

Find an interesting paragraph in one of your books and copy it. Be diligent to make your writing look exactly like it does in the book.

TITLE:_____ **Page Number:_____**

_____

_____

_____

_____

_____

_____

_____

_____

_____

_____

_____

_____

_____

_____

Sketch a Picture

Look through your library books and find something to draw.

Circle
Today's Date

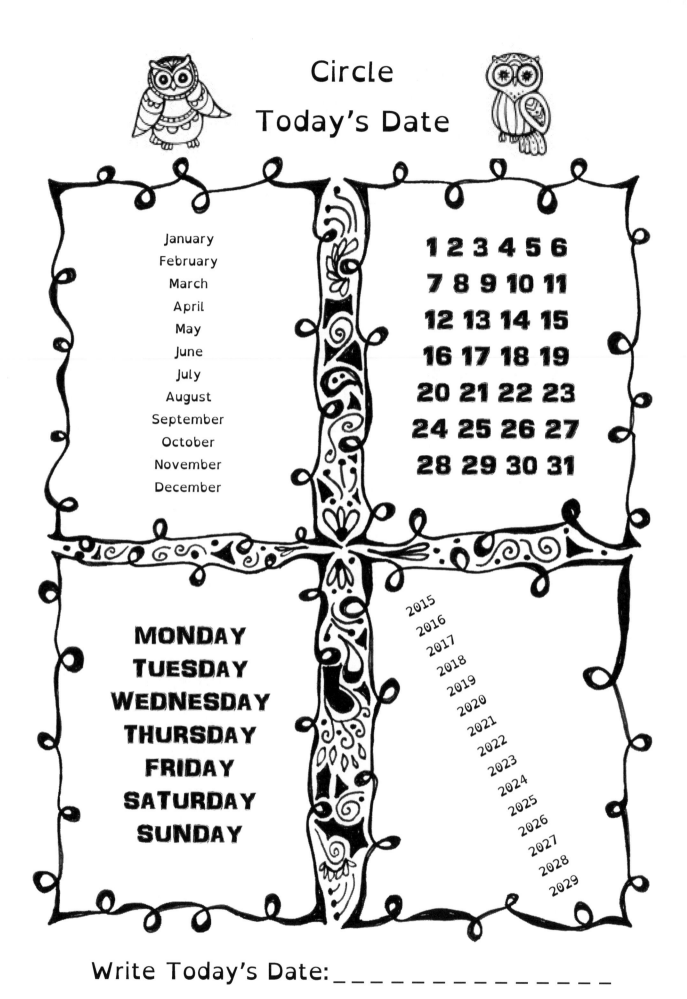

January
February
March
April
May
June
July
August
September
October
November
December

1 2 3 4 5 6
7 8 9 10 11
12 13 14 15
16 17 18 19
20 21 22 23
24 25 26 27
28 29 30 31

MONDAY
TUESDAY
WEDNESDAY
THURSDAY
FRIDAY
SATURDAY
SUNDAY

2015
2016
2017
2018
2019
2020
2021
2022
2023
2024
2025
2026
2027
2028
2029

Write Today's Date: _____

My Thinking Page

This is where you write down your ideas, goals,
and plans - with a thankful heart!

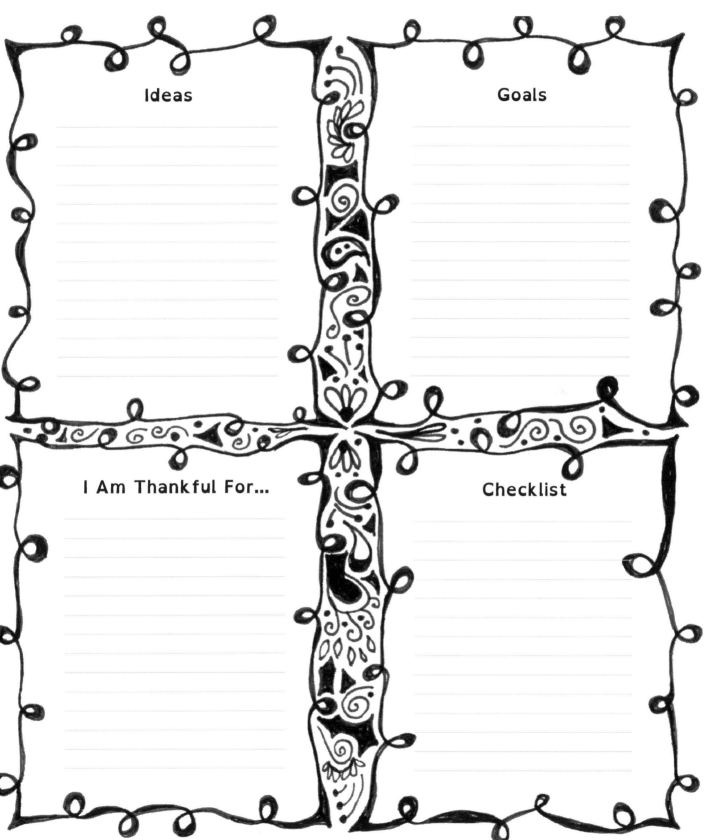

Ideas

Goals

I Am Thankful For...

Checklist

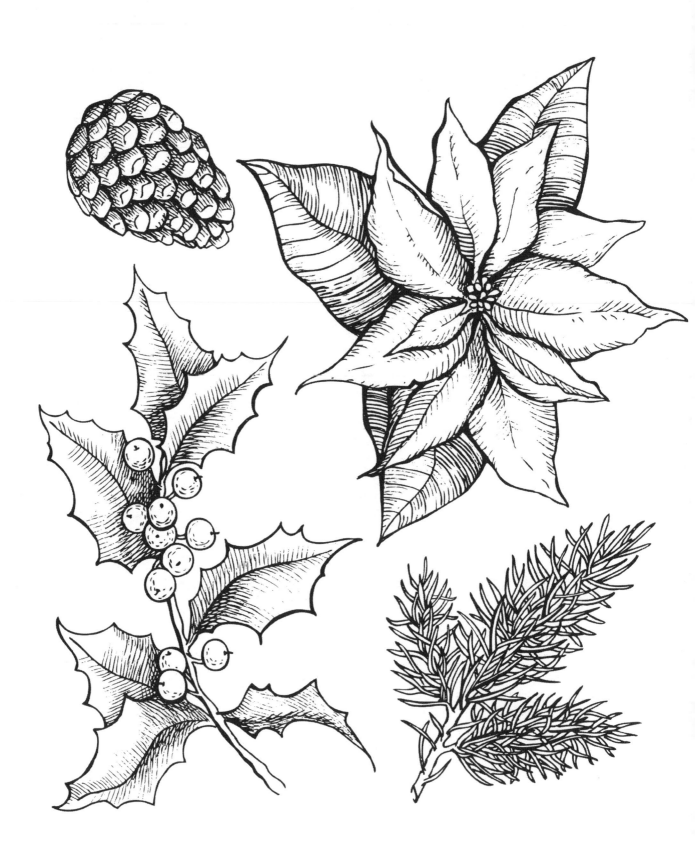

Nature Study

Go outside and make a realistic
drawing of something you find in nature.

Creative Writing

Draw a picture below.

Write a poem or short story about it.

TITLE: _____

_____

_____

_____

_____

_____

_____

_____

_____

_____

_____

_____

_____

_____

My Illustrated TO-DO List

Circle
Today's Date

January	1 2 3 4 5 6
February	7 8 9 10 11
March	12 13 14 15
April	16 17 18 19
May	20 21 22 23
June	24 25 26 27
July	28 29 30 31
August	
September	
October	
November	
December	

MONDAY
TUESDAY
WEDNESDAY
THURSDAY
FRIDAY
SATURDAY
SUNDAY

2015
2016
2017
2018
2019
2020
2021
2022
2023
2024
2025
2026
2027
2028
2029

Write Today's Date: _ _ _ _ _ _ _ _ _ _ _ _ _ _ _ _

Sketch a Picture

Look through your library books and find something to draw.

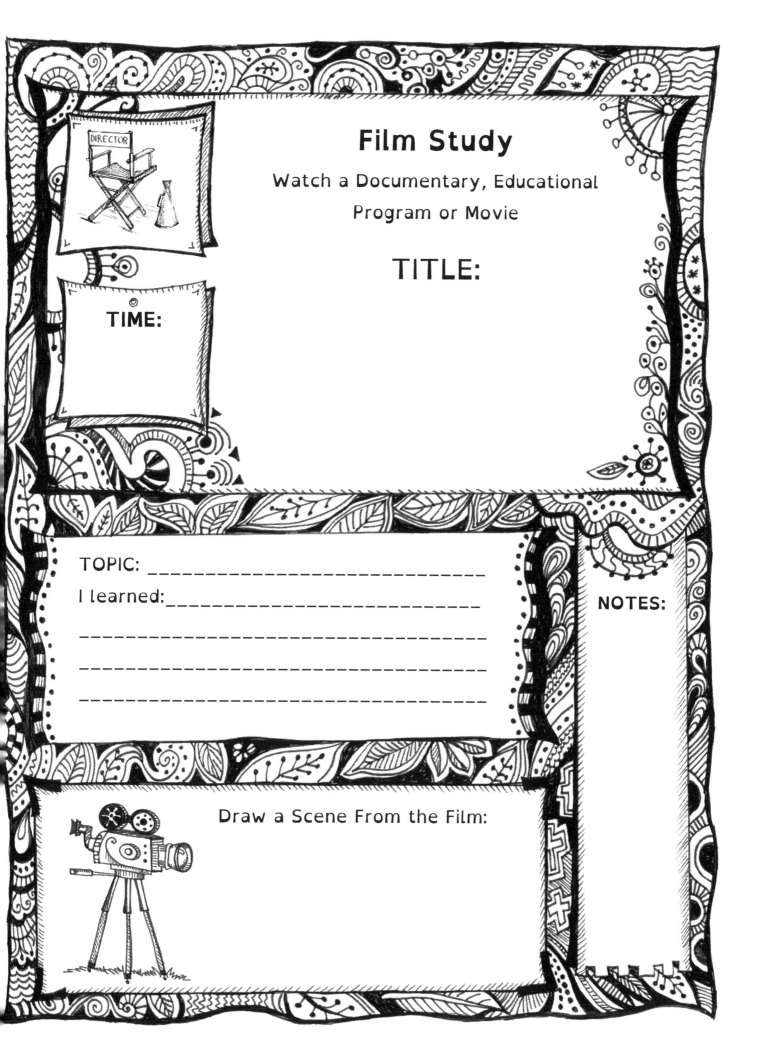

Film Study

Watch a Documentary, Educational Program or Movie

TITLE:

TIME:

TOPIC: _____

I learned:_____

_____

_____

_____

NOTES:

Draw a Scene From the Film:

Write & Draw
about something that
really happened.

_____
_____
_____
_____
_____
_____
_____
_____
_____
_____

Spelling Time

Find 20 Words with 6 letters each.

Look in your books for words.

Write the words here:

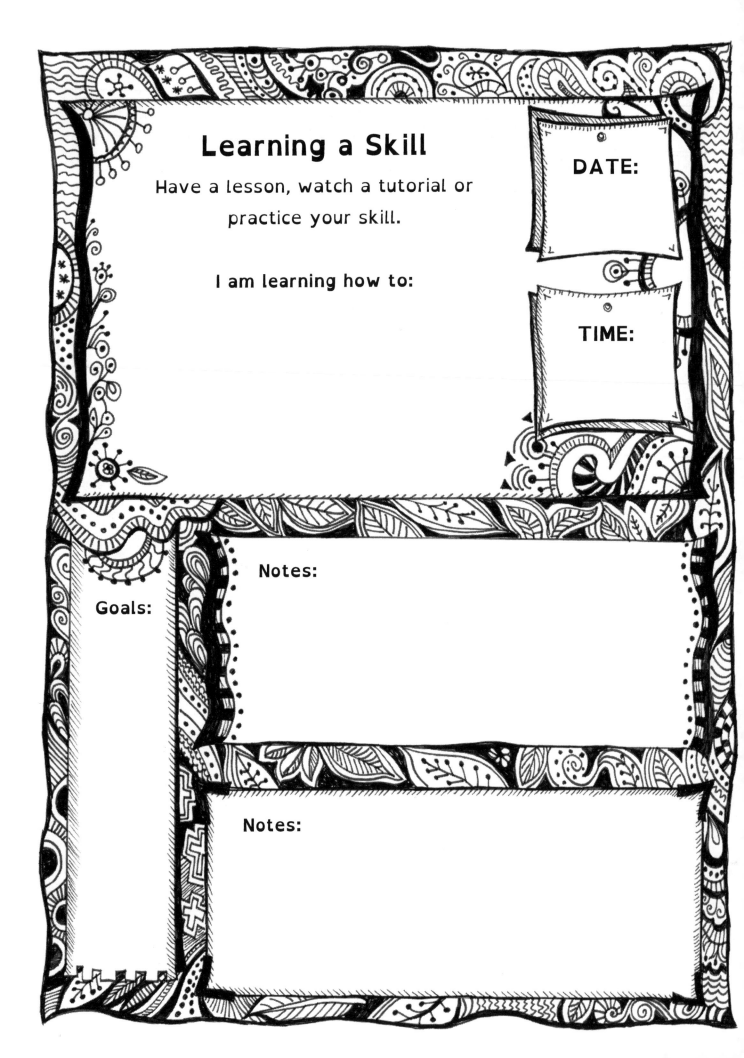

Learning a Skill

Have a lesson, watch a tutorial or practice your skill.

I am learning how to:

DATE:

TIME:

Goals:

Notes:

Notes:

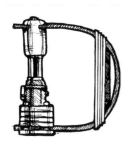

Design Something

Use this graph paper to design something.
If you can't think of anything design a house.

Circle
Today's Date

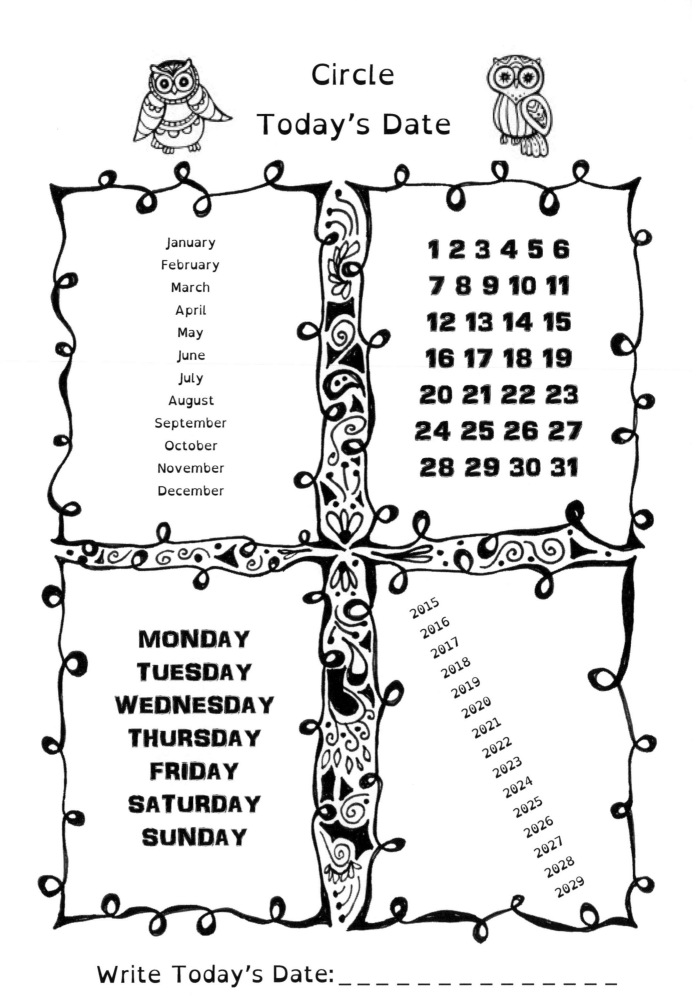

January
February
March
April
May
June
July
August
September
October
November
December

1 2 3 4 5 6
7 8 9 10 11
12 13 14 15
16 17 18 19
20 21 22 23
24 25 26 27
28 29 30 31

MONDAY
TUESDAY
WEDNESDAY
THURSDAY
FRIDAY
SATURDAY
SUNDAY

2015
2016
2017
2018
2019
2020
2021
2022
2023
2024
2025
2026
2027
2028
2029

Write Today's Date: _____

My Thinking Page

This is where you write down your ideas, goals, and plans - with a thankful heart!

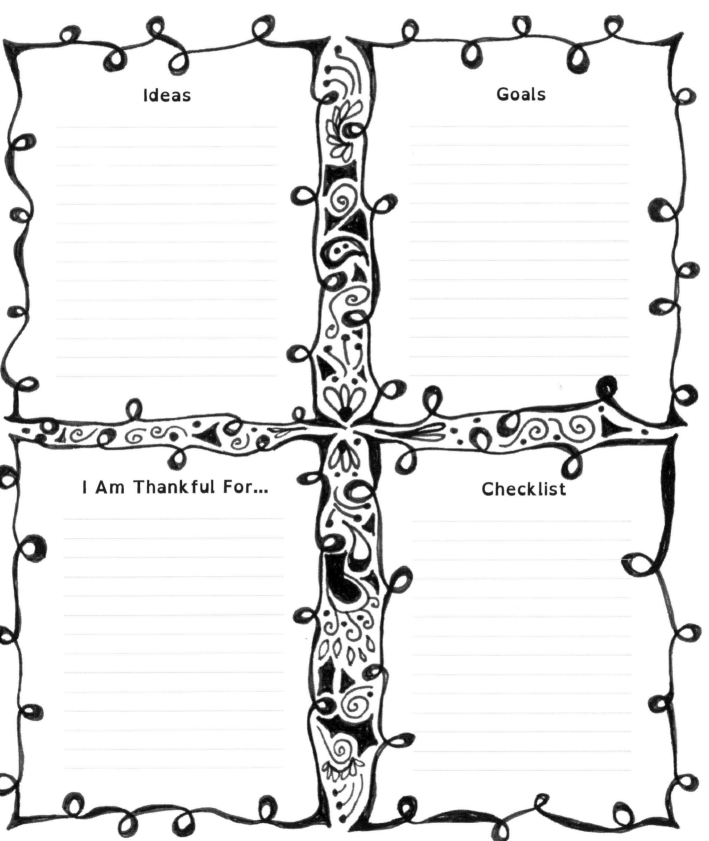

Ideas

Goals

I Am Thankful For...

Checklist

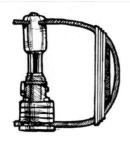

Design Something

Use this graph paper to design something.
If you can't think of anything design a house.

Learning a Skill

Have a lesson, watch a tutorial or practice your skill.

I am learning how to:

DATE:

TIME:

Goals:

Notes:

Notes:

Write & Draw
about something that really happened.

_____

_____

_____

_____

_____

_____

_____

_____

_____

_____

Nature Study

Go outside and make a realistic
drawing of something you find in nature.

Art & Creativity Time

Reading Time - 1 Hour

Choose Four Books - Read from each book for 15 minutes.

Copy a sentence or picture from each book here:

Circle
Today's Date

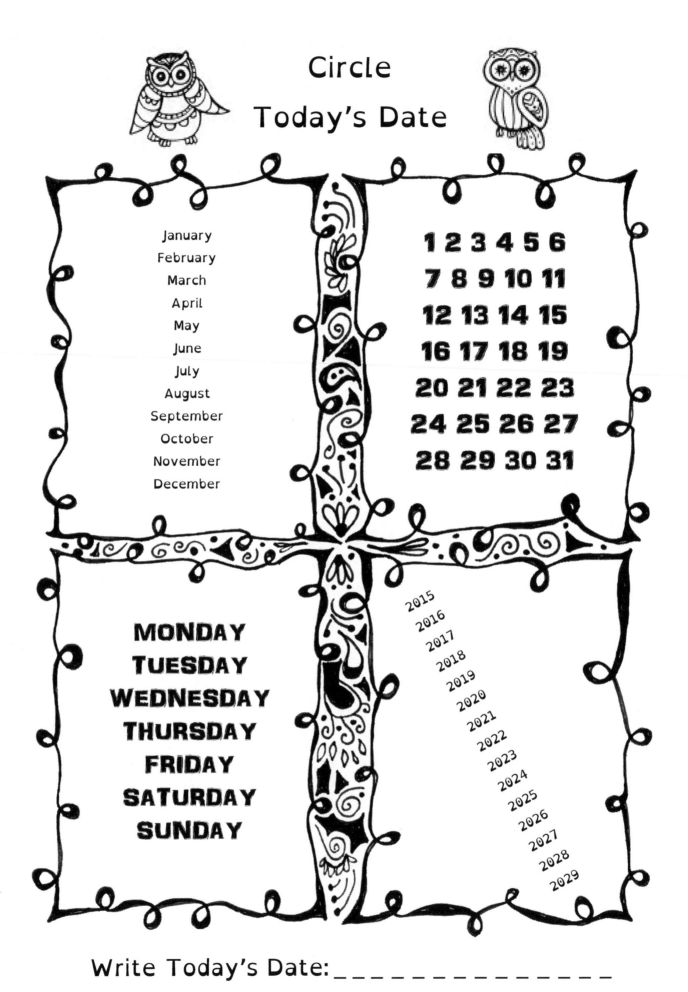

January
February
March
April
May
June
July
August
September
October
November
December

1 2 3 4 5 6
7 8 9 10 11
12 13 14 15
16 17 18 19
20 21 22 23
24 25 26 27
28 29 30 31

MONDAY
TUESDAY
WEDNESDAY
THURSDAY
FRIDAY
SATURDAY
SUNDAY

2015
2016
2017
2018
2019
2020
2021
2022
2023
2024
2025
2026
2027
2028
2029

Write Today's Date: _ _ _ _ _ _ _ _ _ _ _ _ _ _ _ _

My Illustrated TO-DO List

Film Study

Watch a Documentary, Educational Program or Movie

TITLE:

TIME:

TOPIC: _____

I learned:_____

_____

_____

_____

NOTES:

Draw a Scene From the Film:

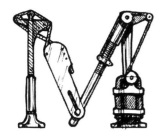

Math Practice

Watch a math tutorial or open up a math book.
You can practice math problems here.

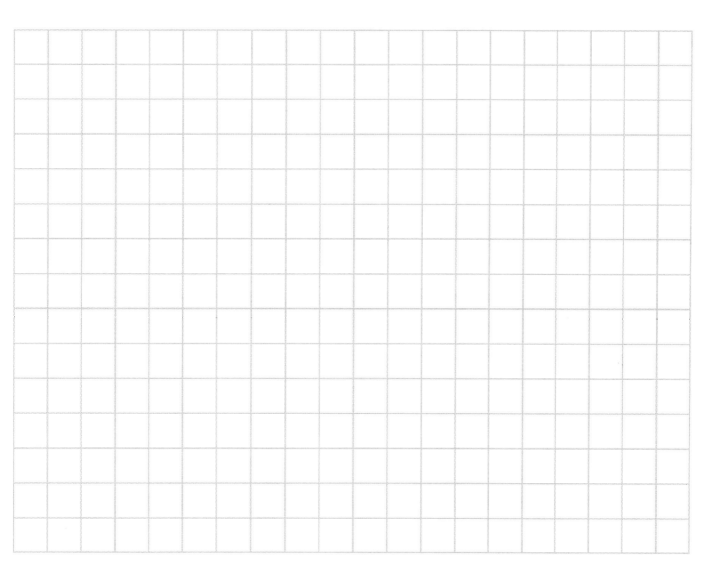

Copywork

Find an interesting paragraph in one of your books and copy it. Be diligent to make your writing look exactly like it does in the book.

TITLE:_____   **Page Number:**_____

_____

_____

_____

_____

_____

_____

_____

_____

_____

_____

_____

_____

_____

_____

_____

Learning a Skill

Have a lesson, watch a tutorial or practice your skill.

I am learning how to:

DATE:

TIME:

Goals:

Notes:

Notes:

Circle
Today's Date

January
February
March
April
May
June
July
August
September
October
November
December

1 2 3 4 5 6
7 8 9 10 11
12 13 14 15
16 17 18 19
20 21 22 23
24 25 26 27
28 29 30 31

MONDAY
TUESDAY
WEDNESDAY
THURSDAY
FRIDAY
SATURDAY
SUNDAY

2015
2016
2017
2018
2019
2020
2021
2022
2023
2024
2025
2026
2027
2028
2029

Write Today's Date: _____

My Thinking Page

This is where you write down your ideas, goals,
and plans - with a thankful heart!

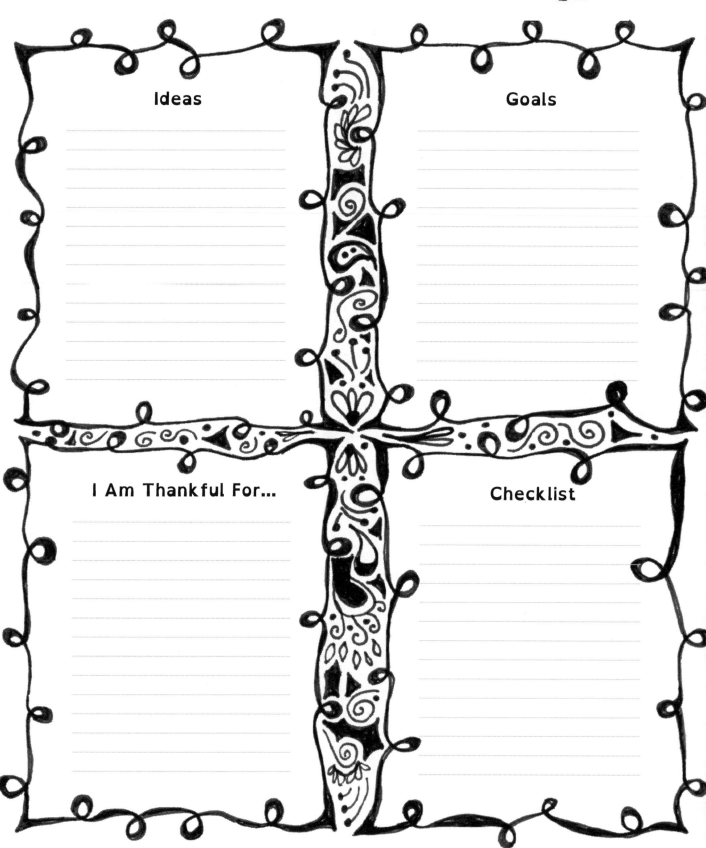

Ideas

Goals

I Am Thankful For...

Checklist

My Illustrated TO-DO List

Write & Draw
about something that
really happened.

_____
_____
_____
_____
_____
_____
_____
_____

Nature Study

Go outside and make a realistic
drawing of something you find in nature.

Reading Time - 1 Hour

Choose Four Books - Read from each book for 15 minutes.

Copy a sentence or picture from each book here:

Circle
Today's Date

January
February
March
April
May
June
July
August
September
October
November
December

1 2 3 4 5 6
7 8 9 10 11
12 13 14 15
16 17 18 19
20 21 22 23
24 25 26 27
28 29 30 31

MONDAY
TUESDAY
WEDNESDAY
THURSDAY
FRIDAY
SATURDAY
SUNDAY

2015
2016
2017
2018
2019
2020
2021
2022
2023
2024
2025
2026
2027
2028
2029

Write Today's Date: _ _ _ _ _ _ _ _ _ _ _ _ _ _ _ _

Spelling Time

Find 20 Words with 5 letters each.

Look in your books for words.

Write the words here:

Film Study

Watch a Documentary, Educational Program or Movie

TITLE:

TIME:

DIRECTOR

TOPIC: _____

I learned:_____

_____

_____

_____

NOTES:

Draw a Scene From the Film:

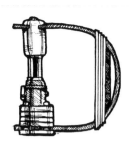

Design Something

Use this graph paper to design something.

If you can't think of anything design a house.

Learning a Skill

Have a lesson, watch a tutorial or practice your skill.

I am learning how to:

DATE:

TIME:

Goals:

Notes:

Notes:

Sketch a Picture

Look through your library books and find something to draw.

Circle
Today's Date

January
February
March
April
May
June
July
August
September
October
November
December

1 2 3 4 5 6
7 8 9 10 11
12 13 14 15
16 17 18 19
20 21 22 23
24 25 26 27
28 29 30 31

MONDAY
TUESDAY
WEDNESDAY
THURSDAY
FRIDAY
SATURDAY
SUNDAY

2015
2016
2017
2018
2019
2020
2021
2022
2023
2024
2025
2026
2027
2028
2029

Write Today's Date: _ _ _ _ _ _ _ _ _ _ _ _ _ _ _ _ _ _ _

My Thinking Page

This is where you write down your ideas, goals, and plans - with a thankful heart!

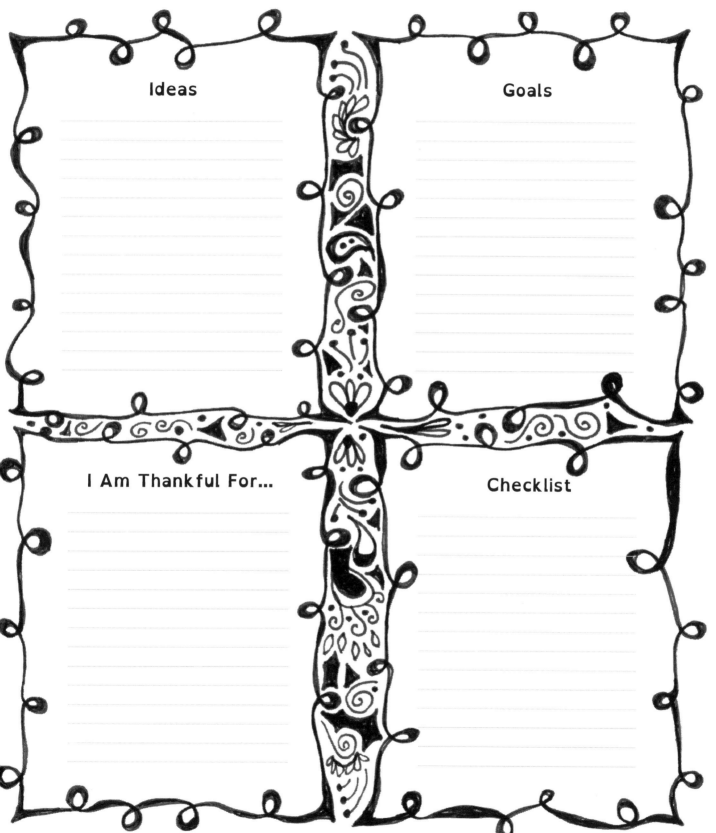

Ideas

Goals

I Am Thankful For...

Checklist

Recipe:

_____

Serves:

Prep Time:

Ingredients:

Instructions:

Shopping List:

Open a cookbook, learn from mom or look online for
some wonderful recipes!

Creative Writing

Draw a picture below.

Write a poem or short story about it.

TITLE: _____

_____

_____

_____

_____

_____

_____

_____

_____

_____

_____

_____

_____

Write & Draw
about something that
really happened.

_____

_____

_____

_____

_____

_____

_____

_____

_____

_____

Nature Study

Go outside and make a realistic
drawing of something you find in nature.

Reading Time - 1 Hour

Choose Four Books - Read from each book for 15 minutes.

Copy a sentence or picture from each book here:

Circle Today's Date

January
February
March
April
May
June
July
August
September
October
November
December

1 2 3 4 5 6
7 8 9 10 11
12 13 14 15
16 17 18 19
20 21 22 23
24 25 26 27
28 29 30 31

MONDAY
TUESDAY
WEDNESDAY
THURSDAY
FRIDAY
SATURDAY
SUNDAY

2015
2016
2017
2018
2019
2020
2021
2022
2023
2024
2025
2026
2027
2028
2029

Write Today's Date: _ _ _ _ _ _ _ _ _ _ _ _ _ _ _ _ _

Spelling Time

Find 20 Words with 4 letters each.
Look in your books for words.
Write the words here:

Film Study

Watch a Documentary, Educational Program or Movie

TITLE:

TIME:

TOPIC: _____

I learned: _____

_____

_____

_____

NOTES:

Draw a Scene From the Film:

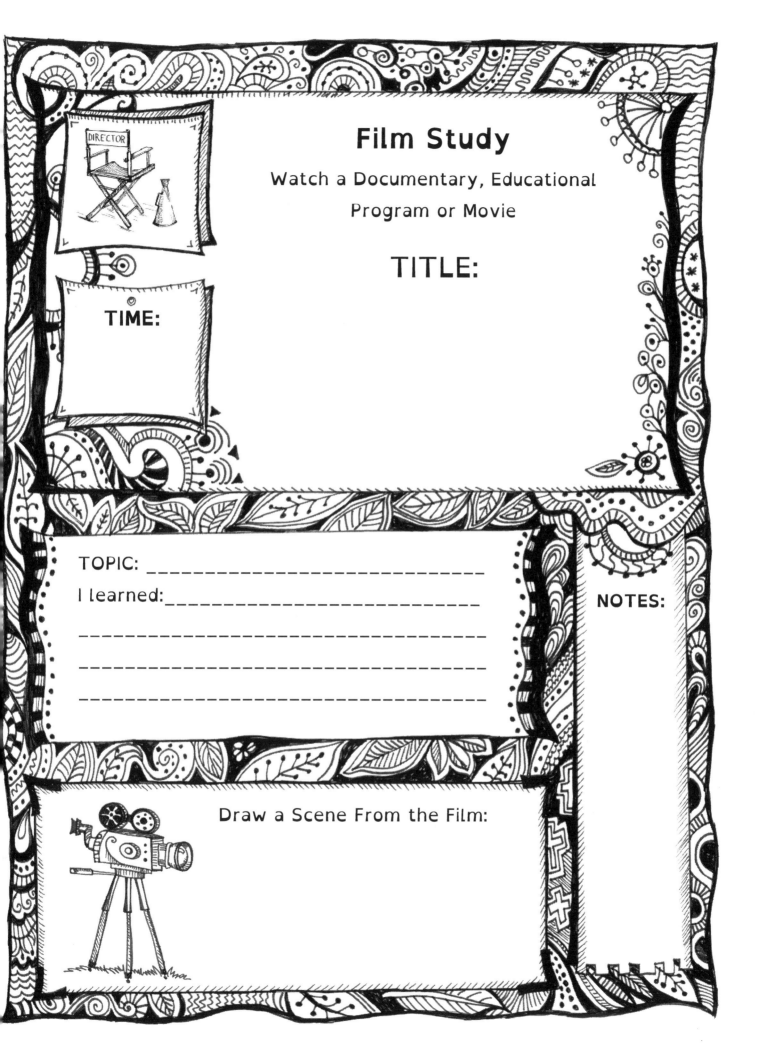

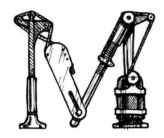

Math Practice

Watch a math tutorial or open up a math book.
You can practice math problems here.

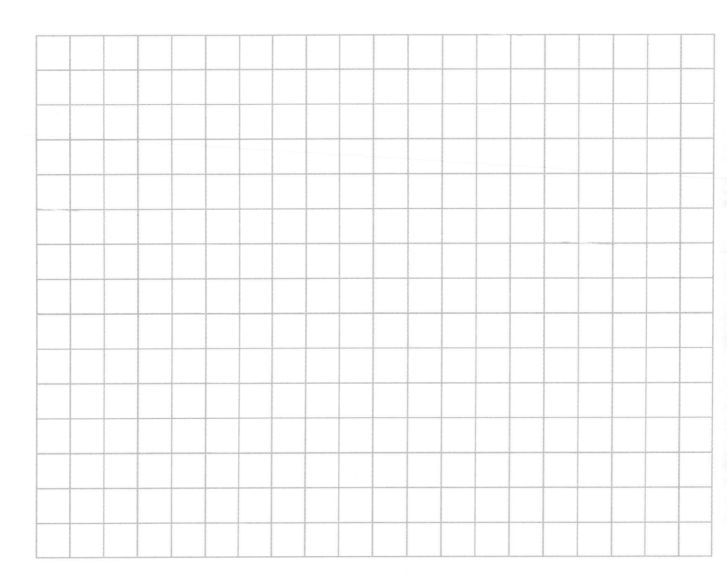

Listening Time

Listen to an audio book or classical music or
ask someone to read a story to you while
you color and draw on the next page.

What are you listening to?

_____

Circle
Today's Date

January
February
March
April
May
June
July
August
September
October
November
December

1 2 3 4 5 6
7 8 9 10 11
12 13 14 15
16 17 18 19
20 21 22 23
24 25 26 27
28 29 30 31

MONDAY
TUESDAY
WEDNESDAY
THURSDAY
FRIDAY
SATURDAY
SUNDAY

2015
2016
2017
2018
2019
2020
2021
2022
2023
2024
2025
2026
2027
2028
2029

Write Today's Date: _ _ _ _ _ _ _ _ _ _ _ _ _ _ _ _ _ _

My Thinking Page

This is where you write down your ideas, goals,
and plans - with a thankful heart!

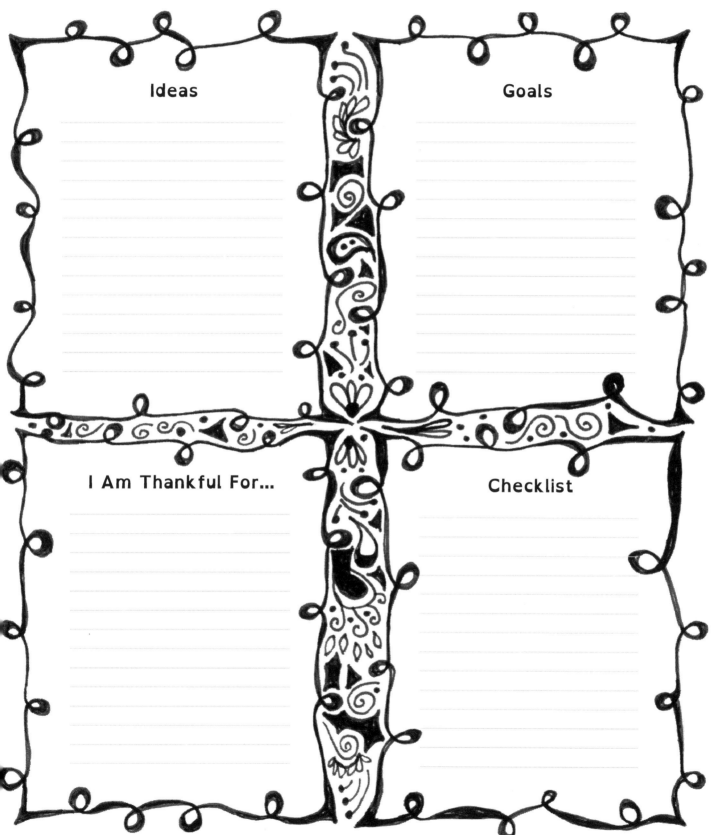

Ideas

Goals

I Am Thankful For...

Checklist

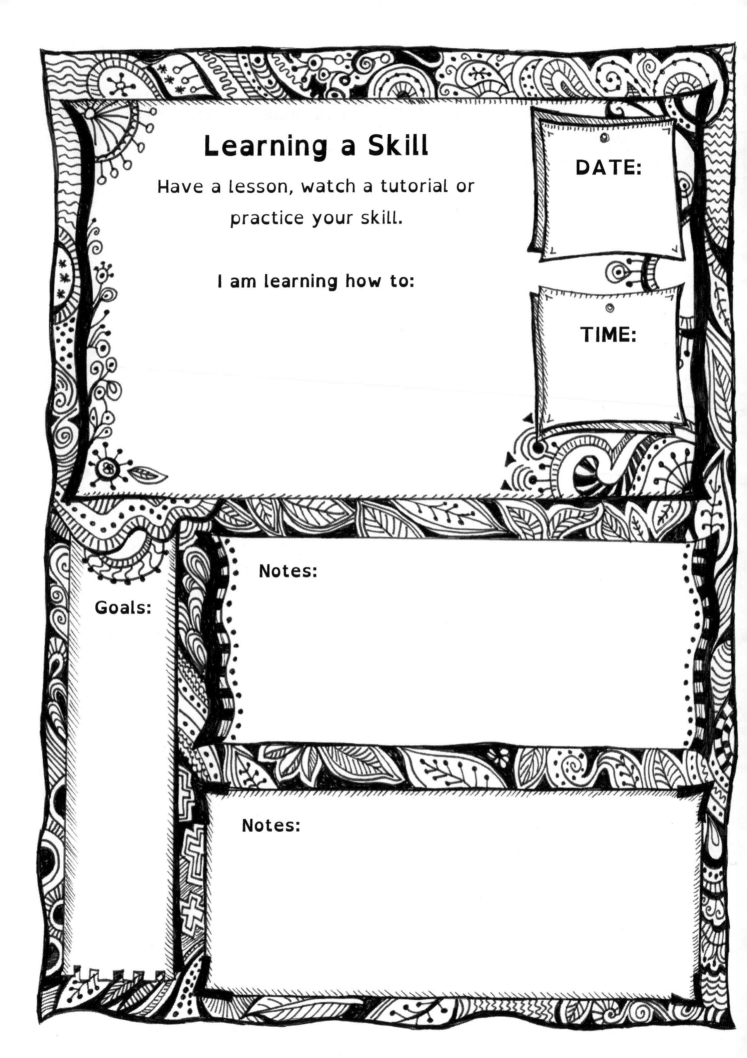

Learning a Skill

Have a lesson, watch a tutorial or practice your skill.

I am learning how to:

DATE:

TIME:

Goals:

Notes:

Notes:

Creative Writing

Draw a picture below.

Write a poem or short story about it.

TITLE: _____

_____
_____
_____
_____
_____
_____
_____
_____
_____
_____
_____
_____
_____
_____

Write & Draw
about something that
really happened.

_____
_____
_____
_____
_____
_____
_____
_____
_____

Nature Study

Go outside and make a realistic
drawing of something you find in nature.

Reading Time - 1 Hour

Choose Four Books - Read from each book for 15 minutes.

Copy a sentence or picture from each book here:

Circle
Today's Date

January
February
March
April
May
June
July
August
September
October
November
December

1 2 3 4 5 6
7 8 9 10 11
12 13 14 15
16 17 18 19
20 21 22 23
24 25 26 27
28 29 30 31

MONDAY
TUESDAY
WEDNESDAY
THURSDAY
FRIDAY
SATURDAY
SUNDAY

2015
2016
2017
2018
2019
2020
2021
2022
2023
2024
2025
2026
2027
2028
2029

Write Today's Date:_____

Spelling Time

Find 20 Words with **3** letters each.

Look in your books for words.

Write the words here:

Film Study

Watch a Documentary, Educational
Program or Movie

TITLE:

TIME:

TOPIC: _____

I learned:_____

_____

_____

_____

NOTES:

Draw a Scene From the Film:

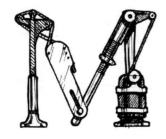

Math Practice

Watch a math tutorial or open up a math book.
You can practice math problems here.

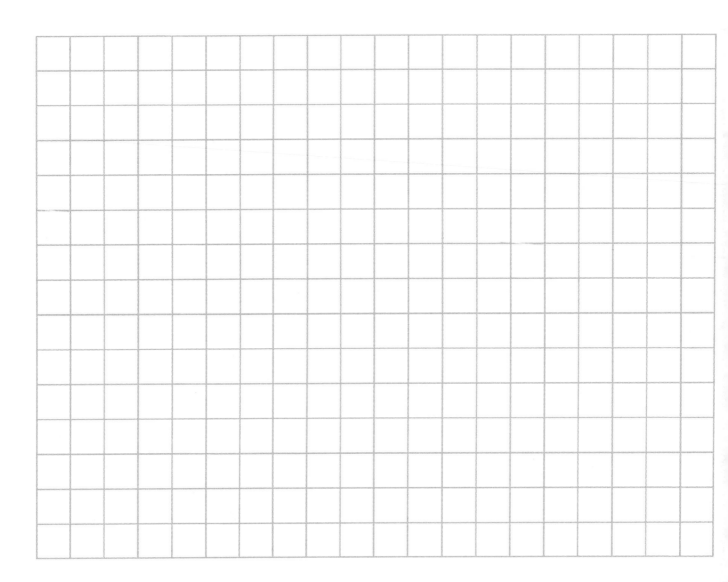

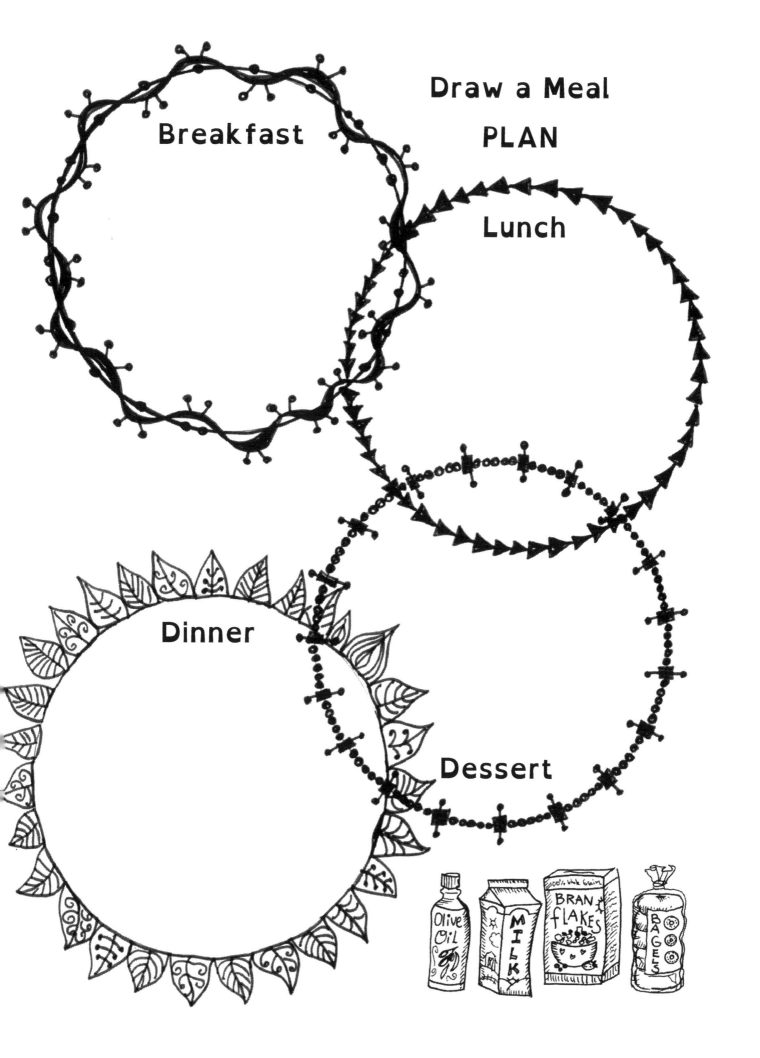

Breakfast

Draw a Meal
PLAN

Lunch

Dinner

Dessert

Copywork

Find an interesting paragraph in one of your books and copy it. Be diligent to make your writing look exactly like it does in the book.

TITLE:_____   **Page Number:**_____

_____

_____

_____

_____

_____

_____

_____

_____

_____

_____

_____

_____

_____

_____

Sketch a Picture

Look through your library books and find something to draw.

Circle
Today's Date

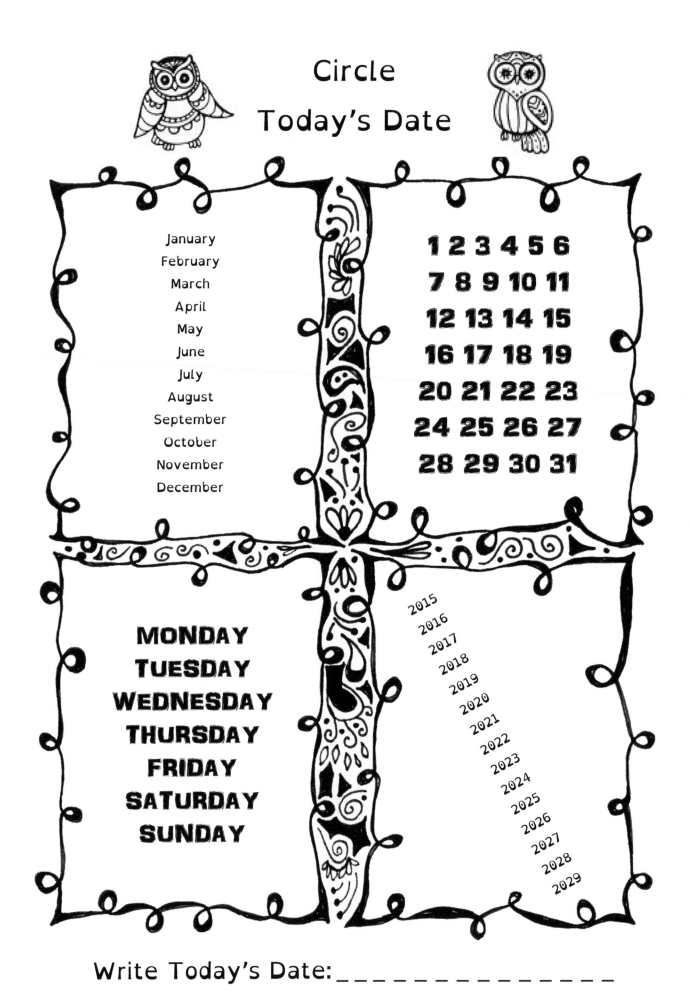

January
February
March
April
May
June
July
August
September
October
November
December

1 2 3 4 5 6
7 8 9 10 11
12 13 14 15
16 17 18 19
20 21 22 23
24 25 26 27
28 29 30 31

MONDAY
TUESDAY
WEDNESDAY
THURSDAY
FRIDAY
SATURDAY
SUNDAY

2015
2016
2017
2018
2019
2020
2021
2022
2023
2024
2025
2026
2027
2028
2029

Write Today's Date: _____

My Thinking Page

This is where you write down your ideas, goals, and plans - with a thankful heart!

Ideas

Goals

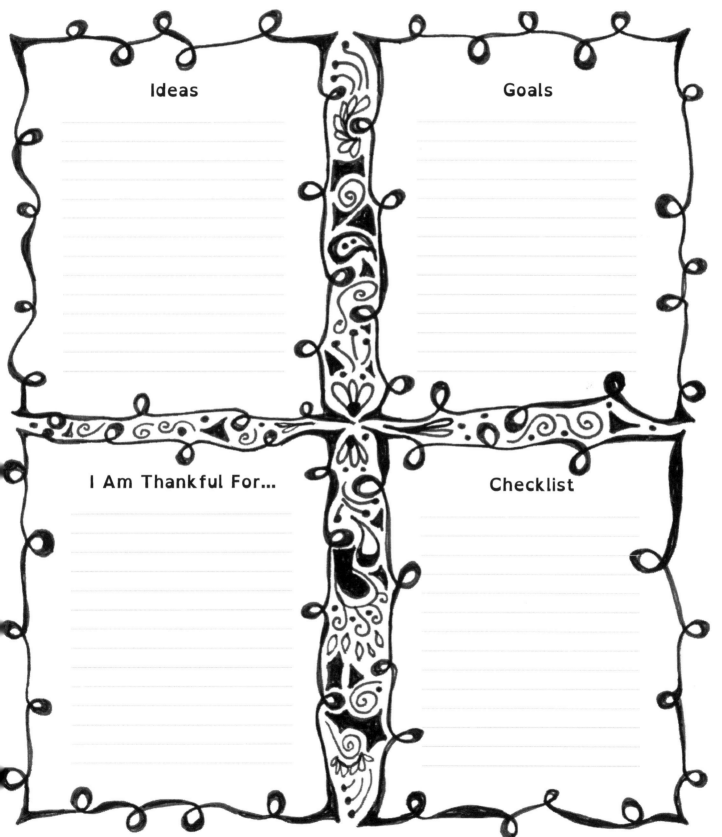

I Am Thankful For...

Checklist

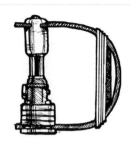

Design Something

Use this graph paper to design something.

If you can't think of anything design a house.

Creative Writing

Draw a picture below.

Write a poem or short story about it.

TITLE: _____

_____
_____
_____
_____
_____
_____
_____
_____
_____
_____
_____
_____
_____
_____

Write & Draw
about something that
really happened.

_____
_____
_____
_____
_____
_____
_____
_____
_____

Nature Study

Go outside and make a realistic drawing of something you find in nature.

Reading Time - 1 Hour

Choose Four Books - Read from each book for 15 minutes.

Copy a sentence or picture from each book here:

Circle
Today's Date

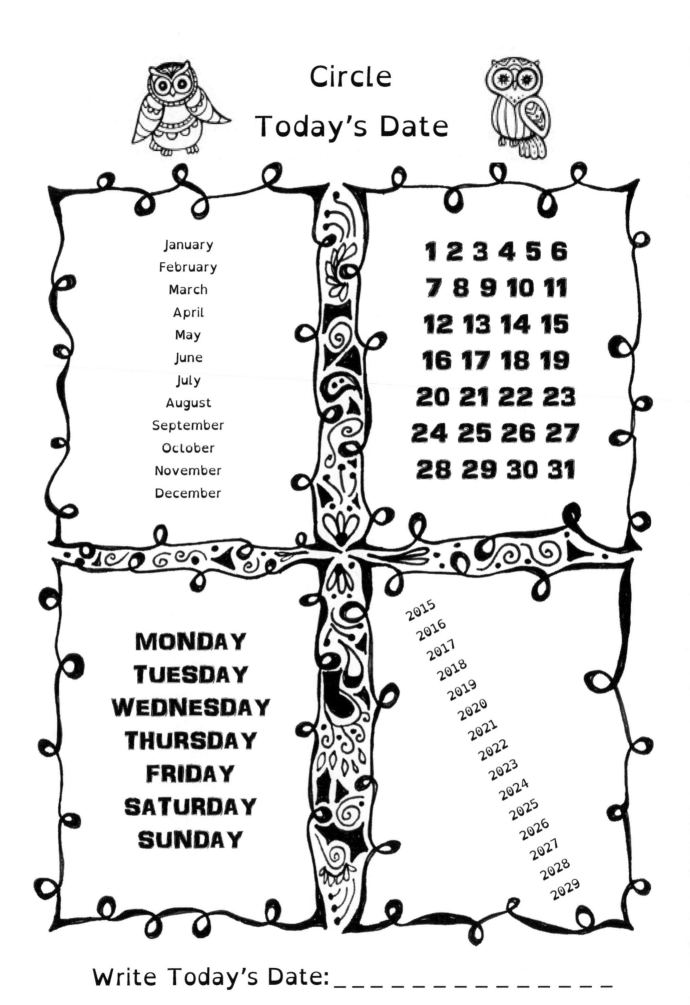

January
February
March
April
May
June
July
August
September
October
November
December

1 2 3 4 5 6
7 8 9 10 11
12 13 14 15
16 17 18 19
20 21 22 23
24 25 26 27
28 29 30 31

MONDAY
TUESDAY
WEDNESDAY
THURSDAY
FRIDAY
SATURDAY
SUNDAY

2015
2016
2017
2018
2019
2020
2021
2022
2023
2024
2025
2026
2027
2028
2029

Write Today's Date:_____

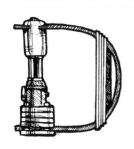

Design Something

Use this graph paper to design something.

If you can't think of anything design a house.

4

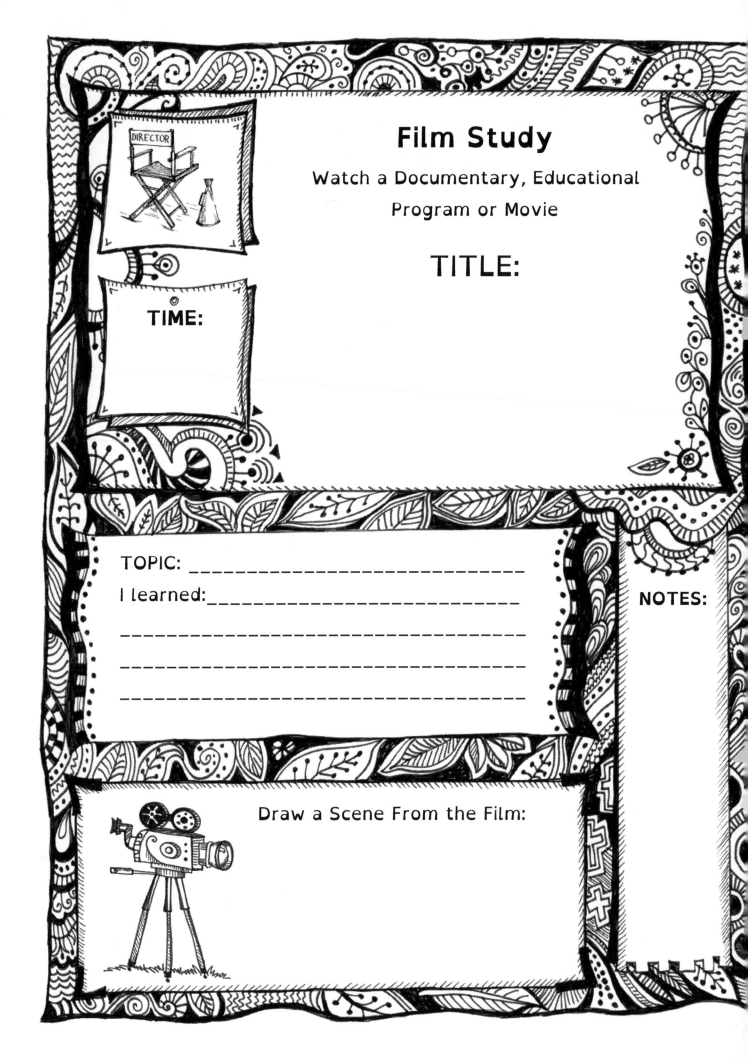

Film Study

Watch a Documentary, Educational Program or Movie

TITLE:

TIME:

TOPIC: _____

I learned: _____

_____

_____

_____

NOTES:

Draw a Scene From the Film:

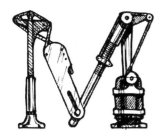

Math Practice

Watch a math tutorial or open up a math book.

You can practice math problems here.

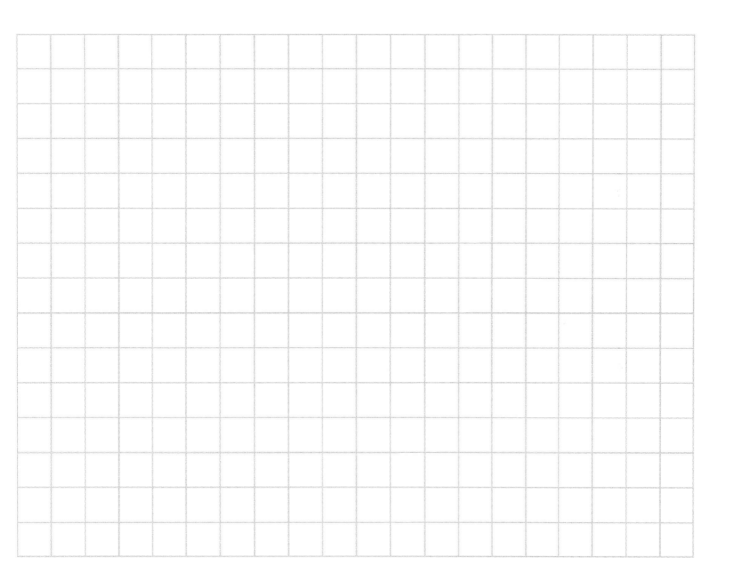

Copywork

Find an interesting paragraph in one of your books and copy it. Be diligent to make your writing look exactly like it does in the book.

TITLE:_____ **Page Number:**_____

_____

_____

_____

_____

_____

_____

_____

_____

_____

_____

_____

_____

_____

_____

_____

_____

Circle
Today's Date

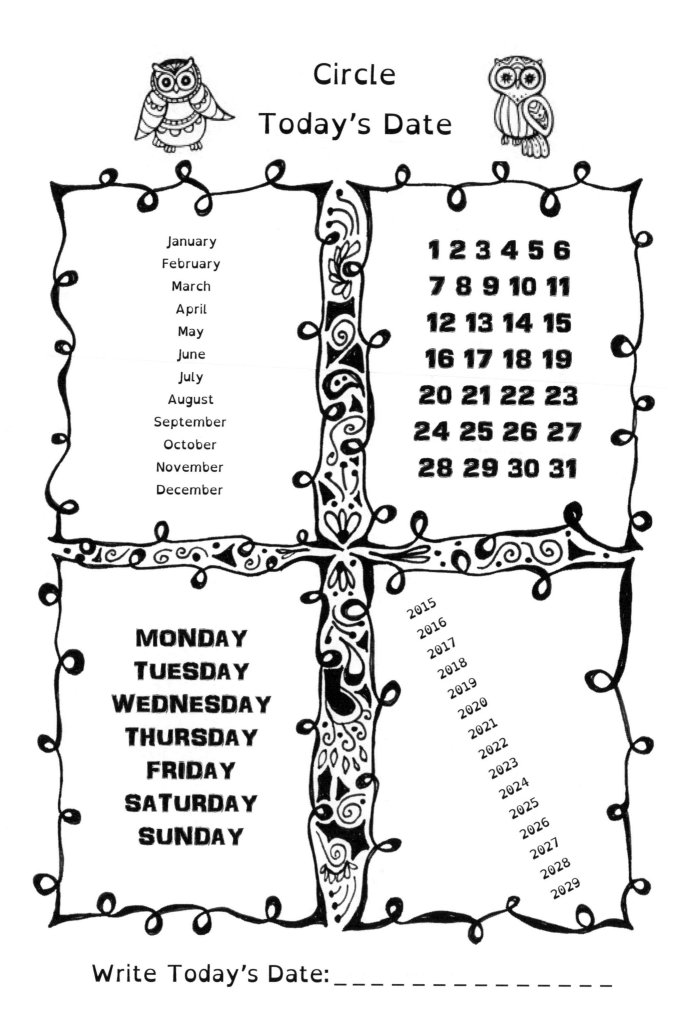

January
February
March
April
May
June
July
August
September
October
November
December

1 2 3 4 5 6
7 8 9 10 11
12 13 14 15
16 17 18 19
20 21 22 23
24 25 26 27
28 29 30 31

MONDAY
TUESDAY
WEDNESDAY
THURSDAY
FRIDAY
SATURDAY
SUNDAY

2015
2016
2017
2018
2019
2020
2021
2022
2023
2024
2025
2026
2027
2028
2029

Write Today's Date:_____

My Thinking Page

This is where you write down your ideas, goals,
and plans - with a thankful heart!

Ideas

Goals

I Am Thankful For...

Checklist

Write & Draw
about something that
really happened.

_____

_____

_____

_____

_____

_____

_____

_____

_____

_____

Nature Study

Go outside and make a realistic
drawing of something you find in nature.

Reading Time - 1 Hour

Choose Four Books - Read from each book for 15 minutes.

Copy a sentence or picture from each book here:

Spelling Time

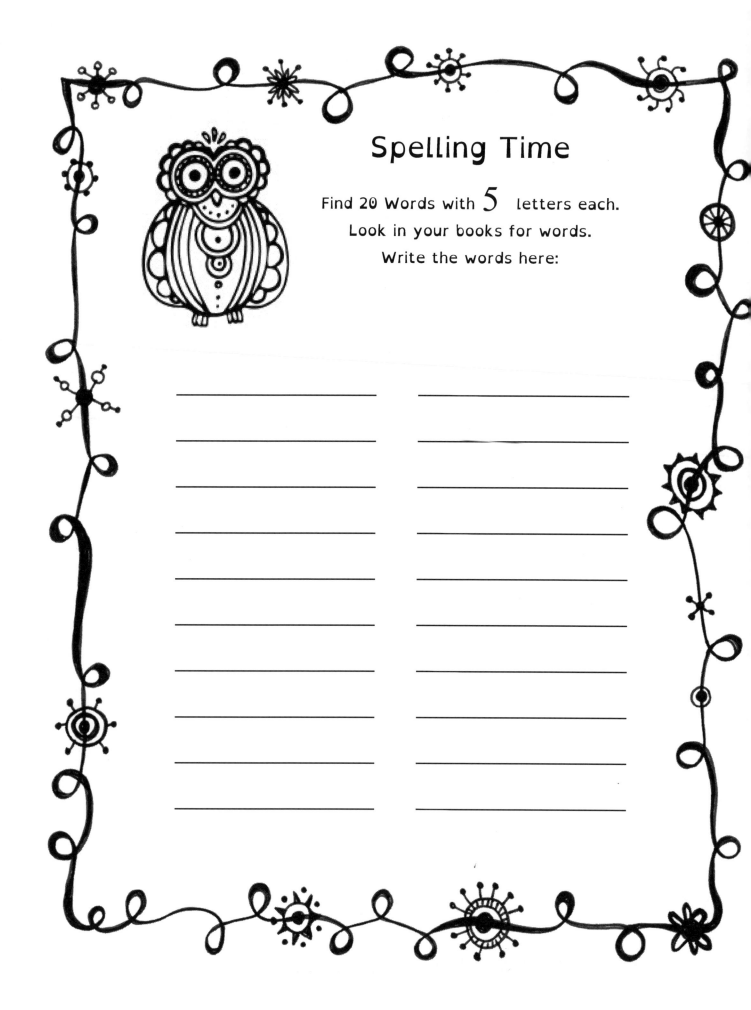

Find 20 Words with 5 letters each.
Look in your books for words.
Write the words here:

_____   _____

_____   _____

_____   _____

_____   _____

_____   _____

_____   _____

_____   _____

_____   _____

Circle
Today's Date

January
February
March
April
May
June
July
August
September
October
November
December

1 2 3 4 5 6
7 8 9 10 11
12 13 14 15
16 17 18 19
20 21 22 23
24 25 26 27
28 29 30 31

MONDAY
TUESDAY
WEDNESDAY
THURSDAY
FRIDAY
SATURDAY
SUNDAY

2015
2016
2017
2018
2019
2020
2021
2022
2023
2024
2025
2026
2027
2028
2029

Write Today's Date: _ _ _ _ _ _ _ _ _ _ _ _ _ _ _ _

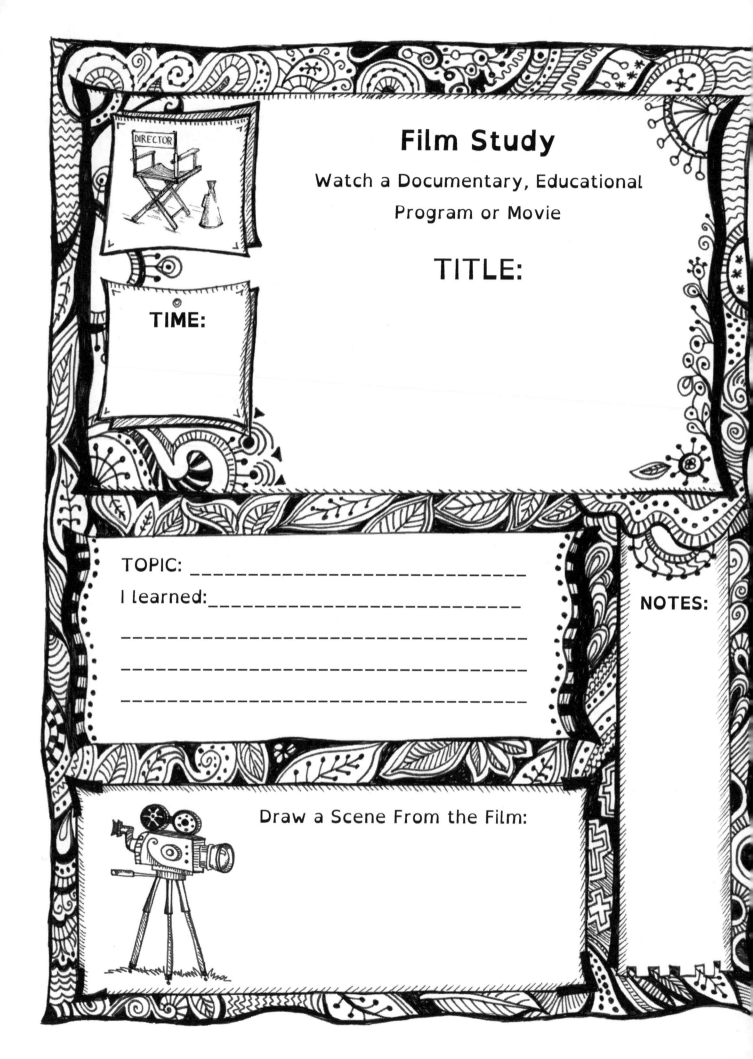

Film Study

Watch a Documentary, Educational
Program or Movie

TITLE:

DIRECTOR

TIME:

TOPIC: _____

I learned:_____

_____

_____

_____

NOTES:

Draw a Scene From the Film:

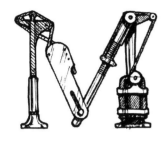

Math Practice

Watch a math tutorial or open up a math book.

You can practice math problems here.

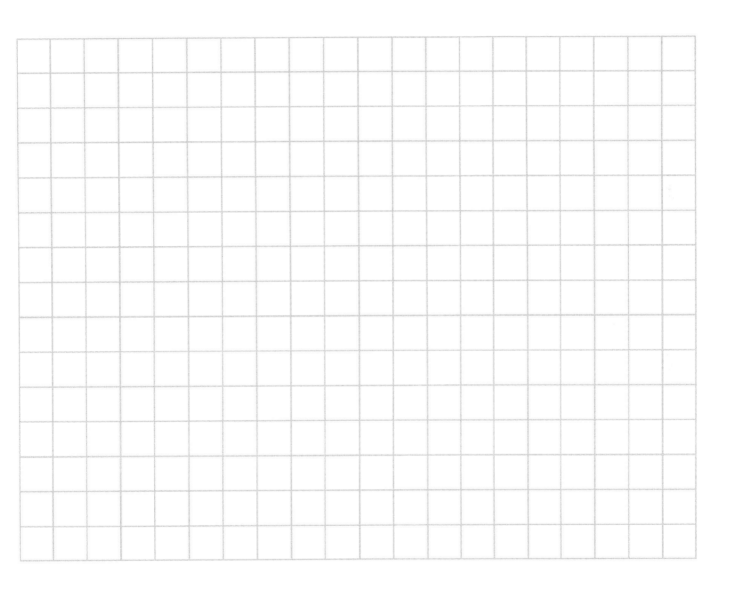

Fun Writing Practice:

ABCDEFGHIJKLMNOPQURSTUVWXYZ

abcdefghijklmnopqrstuvwxyz

ABCDEFGHIJKLMNOPQURSTUVWXYZ

ABCDEFGHIJKLMNOPQURSTUVWXYZ

abcdefghijklmnopqrstuvwxyz

Copywork

Find an interesting paragraph in one of your books and copy it. Be diligent to make your writing look exactly like it does in the book.

TITLE:_____ **Page Number:**_____

_____

_____

_____

_____

_____

_____

_____

_____

_____

_____

_____

_____

_____

_____

_____

Circle
Today's Date

January
February
March
April
May
June
July
August
September
October
November
December

1 2 3 4 5 6
7 8 9 10 11
12 13 14 15
16 17 18 19
20 21 22 23
24 25 26 27
28 29 30 31

MONDAY
TUESDAY
WEDNESDAY
THURSDAY
FRIDAY
SATURDAY
SUNDAY

2015
2016
2017
2018
2019
2020
2021
2022
2023
2024
2025
2026
2027
2028
2029

Write Today's Date: _ _ _ _ _ _ _ _ _ _ _ _ _ _ _ _ _

My Thinking Page

This is where you write down your ideas, goals, and plans - with a thankful heart!

Ideas

Goals

I Am Thankful For...

Checklist

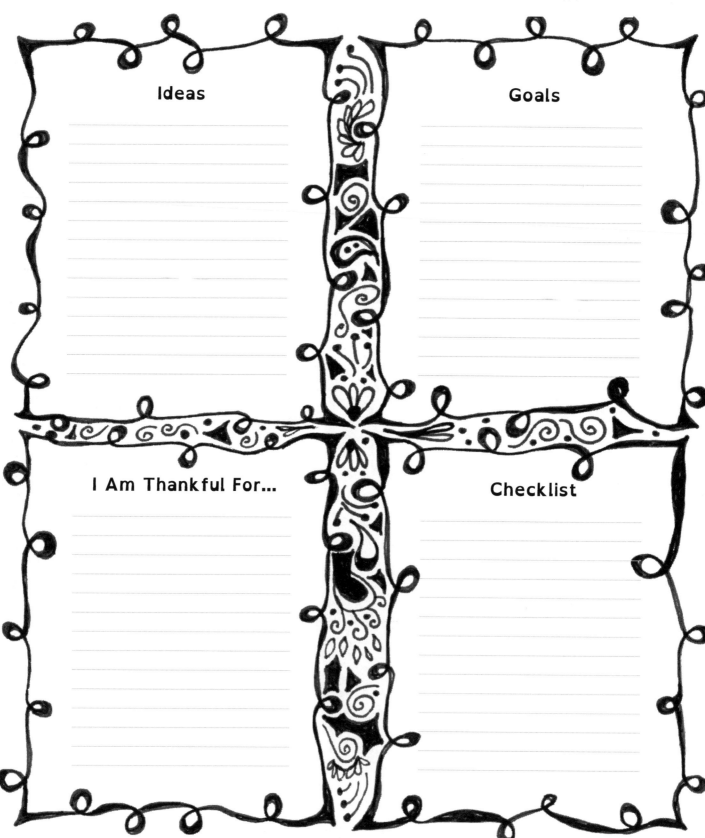

Write & Draw
about something that
really happened.

_____

_____

_____

_____

_____

_____

_____

_____

_____

Nature Study

Go outside and make a realistic drawing of something you find in nature.

Reading Time - 1 Hour

Choose Four Books - Read from each book for 15 minutes.

Copy a sentence or picture from each book here:

Circle
Today's Date

January
February
March
April
May
June
July
August
September
October
November
December

1 2 3 4 5 6
7 8 9 10 11
12 13 14 15
16 17 18 19
20 21 22 23
24 25 26 27
28 29 30 31

MONDAY
TUESDAY
WEDNESDAY
THURSDAY
FRIDAY
SATURDAY
SUNDAY

2015
2016
2017
2018
2019
2020
2021
2022
2023
2024
2025
2026
2027
2028
2029

Write Today's Date: _ _ _ _ _ _ _ _ _ _ _ _ _ _ _ _

Spelling Time

Find 20 Words with 6 letters each.
Look in your books for words.
Write the words here:

Film Study

Watch a Documentary, Educational Program or Movie

TITLE:

TIME:

TOPIC: _____

I learned: _____

_____

_____

_____

NOTES:

Draw a Scene From the Film:

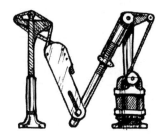

Math Practice

Watch a math tutorial or open up a math book.
You can practice math problems here.

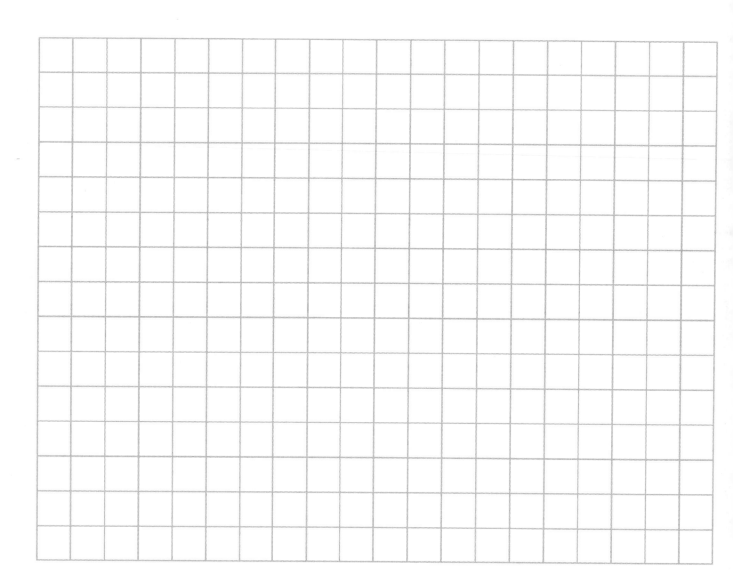

My Illustrated TO-DO List

Copywork

Find an interesting paragraph in one of your books and copy it. Be diligent to make your writing look exactly like it does in the book.

TITLE:_____ **Page Number:**_____

_____

_____

_____

_____

_____

_____

_____

_____

_____

_____

_____

_____

_____

_____

_____

Sketch a Picture

Look through your library books and find something to draw.

Circle
Today's Date

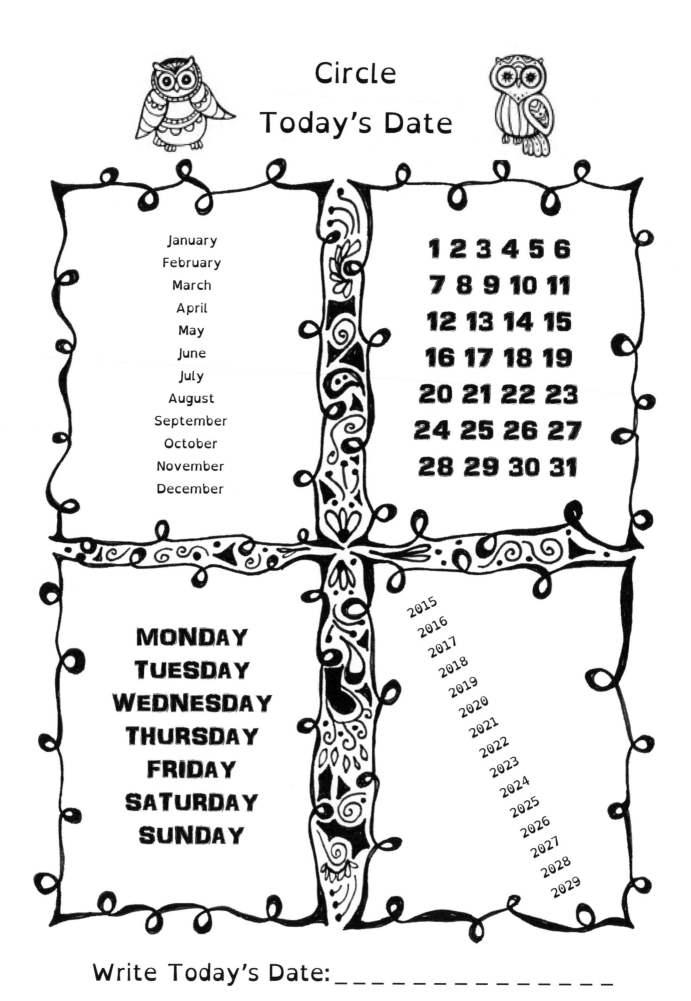

January	1 2 3 4 5 6
February	7 8 9 10 11
March	12 13 14 15
April	16 17 18 19
May	20 21 22 23
June	24 25 26 27
July	28 29 30 31
August	
September	
October	
November	
December	

MONDAY	2015
TUESDAY	2016
WEDNESDAY	2017
THURSDAY	2018
FRIDAY	2019
SATURDAY	2020
SUNDAY	2021
	2022
	2023
	2024
	2025
	2026
	2027
	2028
	2029

Write Today's Date:_____

My Thinking Page

This is where you write down your ideas, goals,
and plans - with a thankful heart!

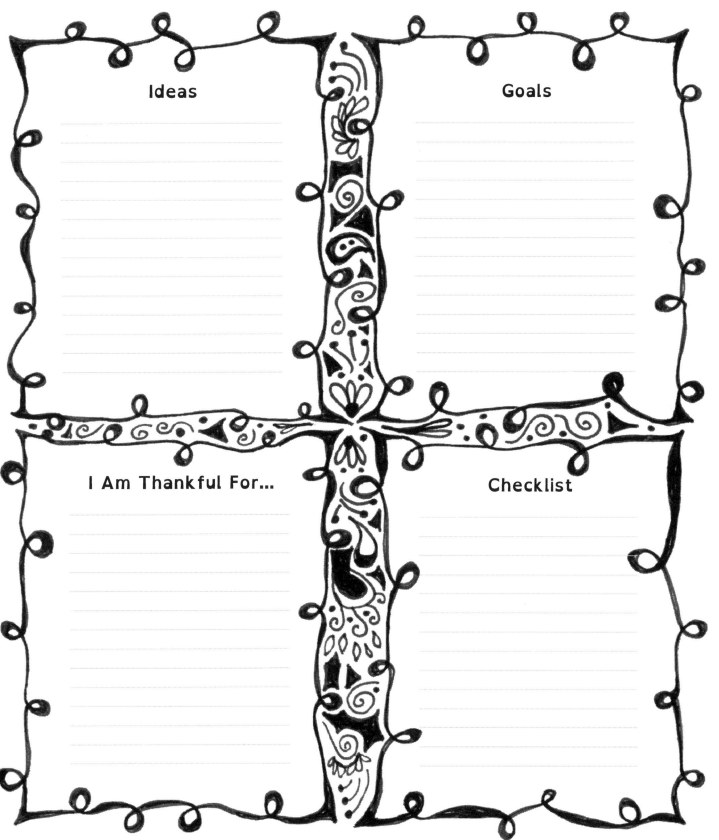

Ideas

Goals

I Am Thankful For...

Checklist

Creative Writing

Draw a picture below.
Write a poem or short story about it.

TITLE: _____

_____
_____
_____
_____
_____
_____
_____
_____
_____
_____
_____
_____
_____
_____

Nature Study

Go outside and make a realistic
drawing of something you find in nature.

Reading Time - 1 Hour

Choose Four Books - Read from each book for 15 minutes.

Copy a sentence or picture from each book here:

Circle Today's Date

January
February
March
April
May
June
July
August
September
October
November
December

1 2 3 4 5 6
7 8 9 10 11
12 13 14 15
16 17 18 19
20 21 22 23
24 25 26 27
28 29 30 31

MONDAY
TUESDAY
WEDNESDAY
THURSDAY
FRIDAY
SATURDAY
SUNDAY

2015
2016
2017
2018
2019
2020
2021
2022
2023
2024
2025
2026
2027
2028
2029

Write Today's Date:_____

Spelling Time

Find 20 Words with 7 letters each.
Look in your books for words.
Write the words here:

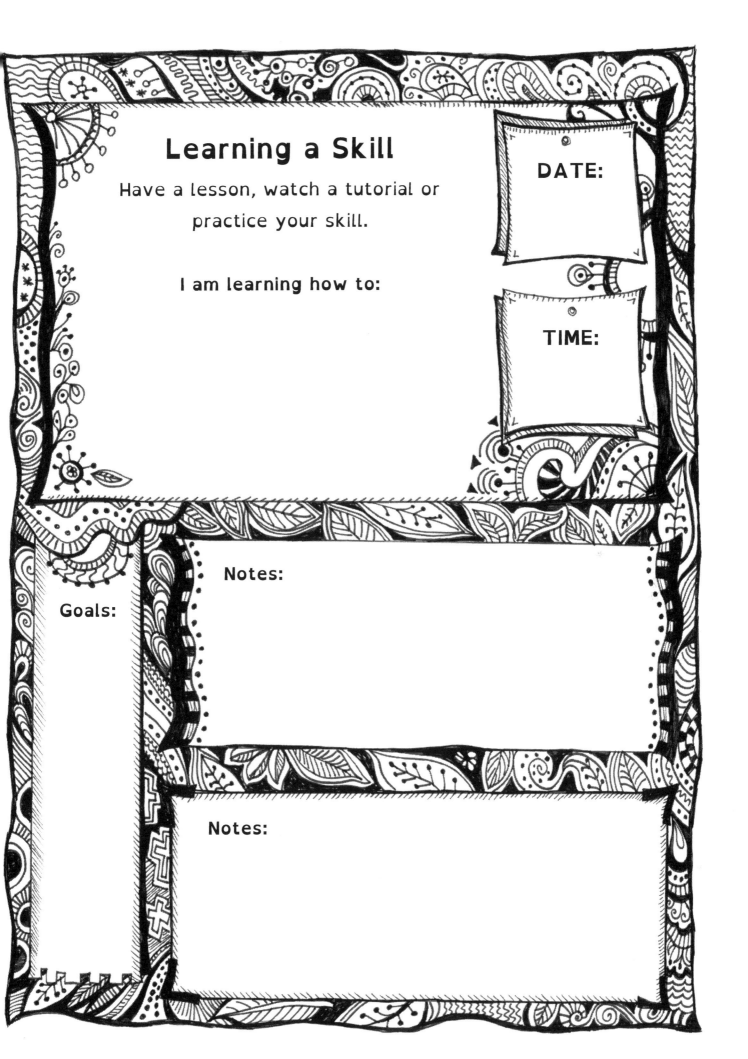

Learning a Skill

Have a lesson, watch a tutorial or practice your skill.

I am learning how to:

DATE:

TIME:

Goals:

Notes:

Notes:

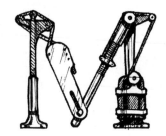

Math Practice

Watch a math tutorial or open up a math book.

You can practice math problems here.

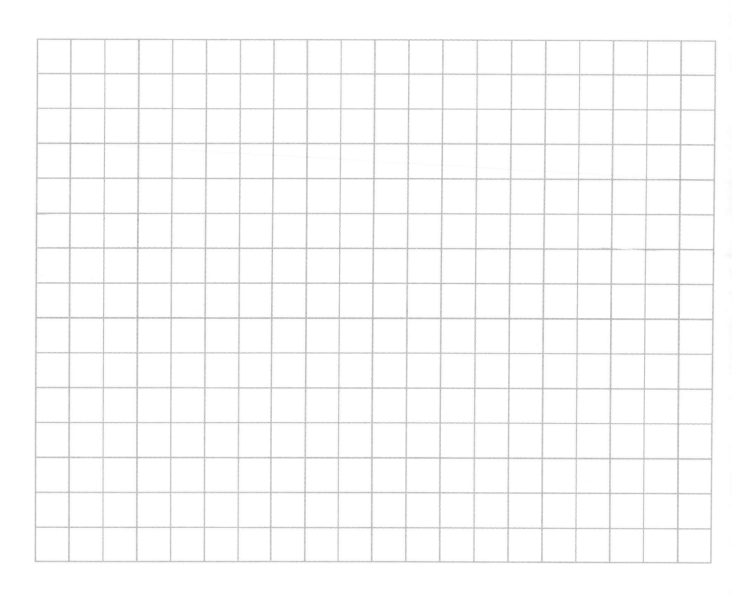

Copywork

Find an interesting paragraph in one of your books and copy it. Be diligent to make your writing look exactly like it does in the book.

TITLE:_____ **Page Number:**_____

_____

_____

_____

_____

_____

_____

_____

_____

_____

_____

_____

_____

_____

_____

_____

Circle Today's Date

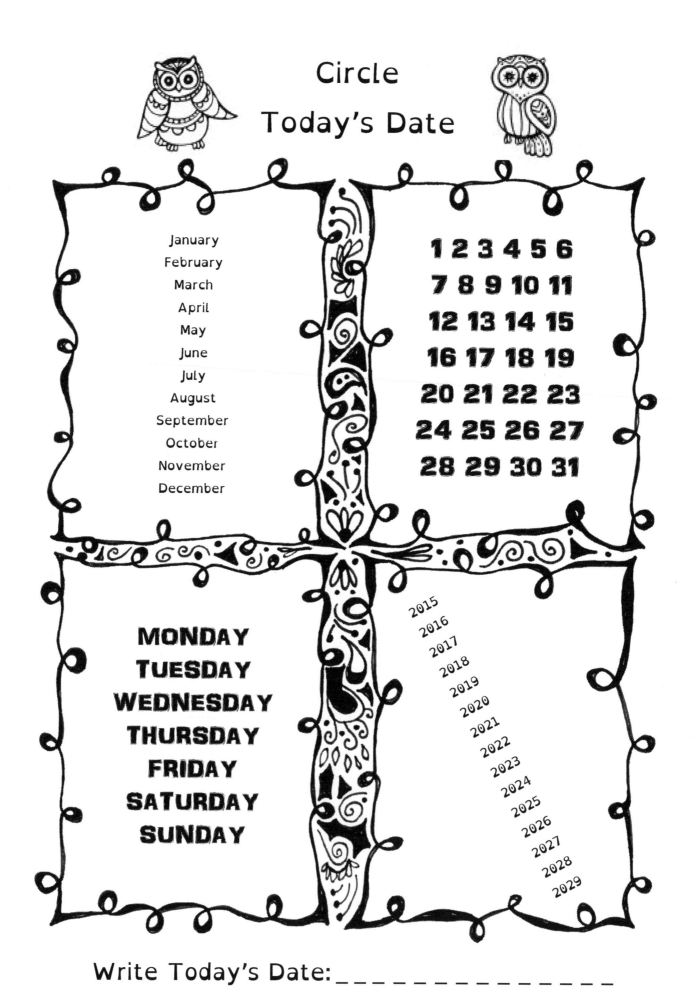

January
February
March
April
May
June
July
August
September
October
November
December

1 2 3 4 5 6
7 8 9 10 11
12 13 14 15
16 17 18 19
20 21 22 23
24 25 26 27
28 29 30 31

MONDAY
TUESDAY
WEDNESDAY
THURSDAY
FRIDAY
SATURDAY
SUNDAY

2015
2016
2017
2018
2019
2020
2021
2022
2023
2024
2025
2026
2027
2028
2029

Write Today's Date: _ _ _ _ _ _ _ _ _ _ _ _ _ _ _ _ _

My Thinking Page

This is where you write down your ideas, goals,
and plans - with a thankful heart!

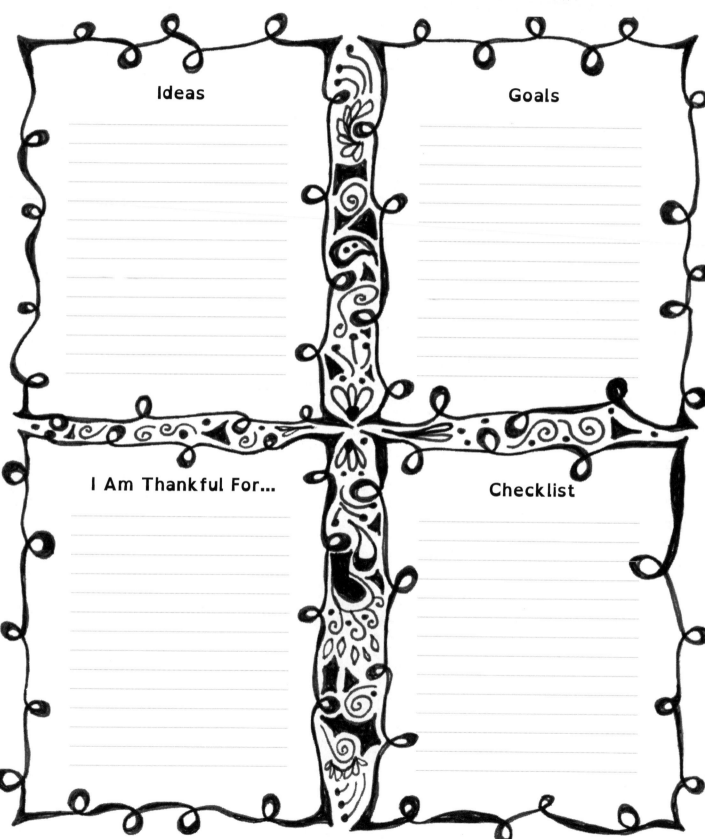

Ideas

Goals

I Am Thankful For...

Checklist

Creative Writing

Draw a picture below.

Write a poem or short story about it.

TITLE: _____

_____
_____
_____
_____
_____
_____
_____
_____
_____
_____
_____
_____
_____
_____

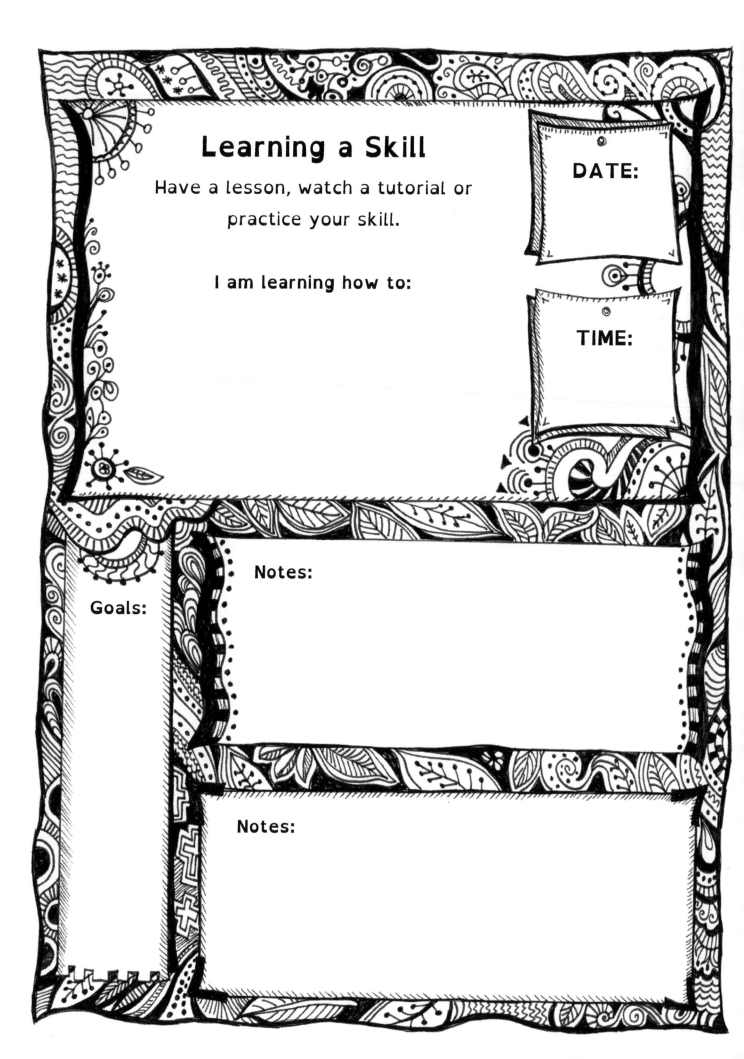

Learning a Skill

Have a lesson, watch a tutorial or practice your skill.

I am learning how to:

DATE:

TIME:

Goals:

Notes:

Notes:

Nature Study

Go outside and make a realistic
drawing of something you find in nature.

Reading Time - 1 Hour

Choose Four Books - Read from each book for 15 minutes.
Copy a sentence or picture from each book here:

Circle
Today's Date

January	1 2 3 4 5 6
February	7 8 9 10 11
March	12 13 14 15
April	16 17 18 19
May	20 21 22 23
June	24 25 26 27
July	28 29 30 31
August	
September	
October	
November	
December	

MONDAY
TUESDAY
WEDNESDAY
THURSDAY
FRIDAY
SATURDAY
SUNDAY

2015
2016
2017
2018
2019
2020
2021
2022
2023
2024
2025
2026
2027
2028
2029

Write Today's Date: _ _ _ _ _ _ _ _ _ _ _ _ _ _ _ _

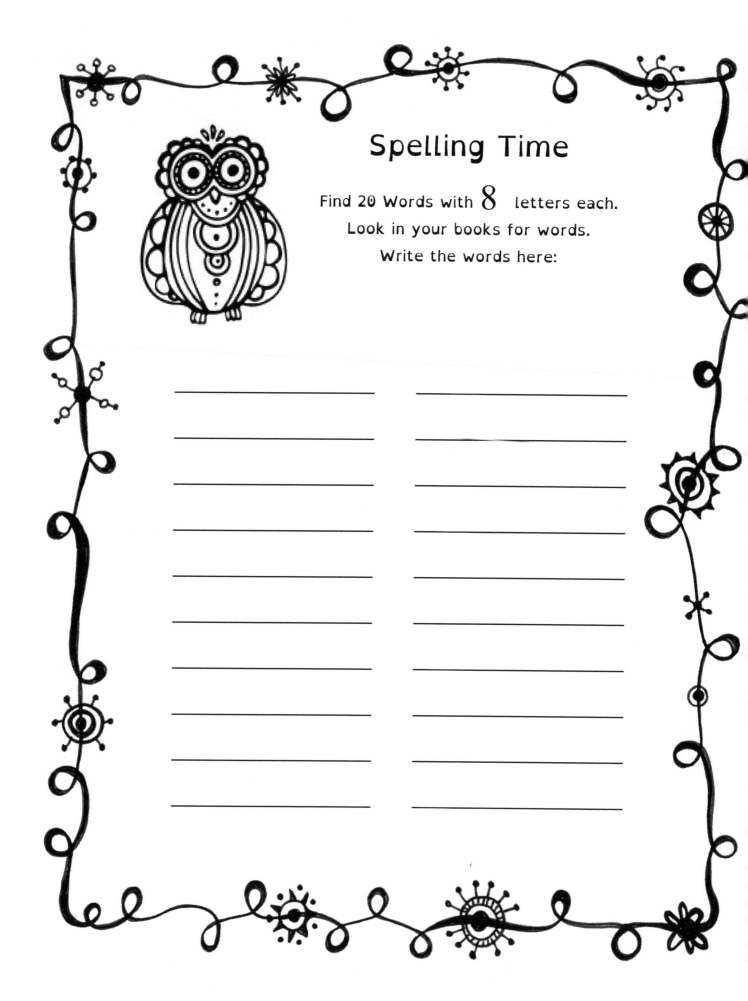

Spelling Time

Find 20 Words with 8 letters each.

Look in your books for words.

Write the words here:

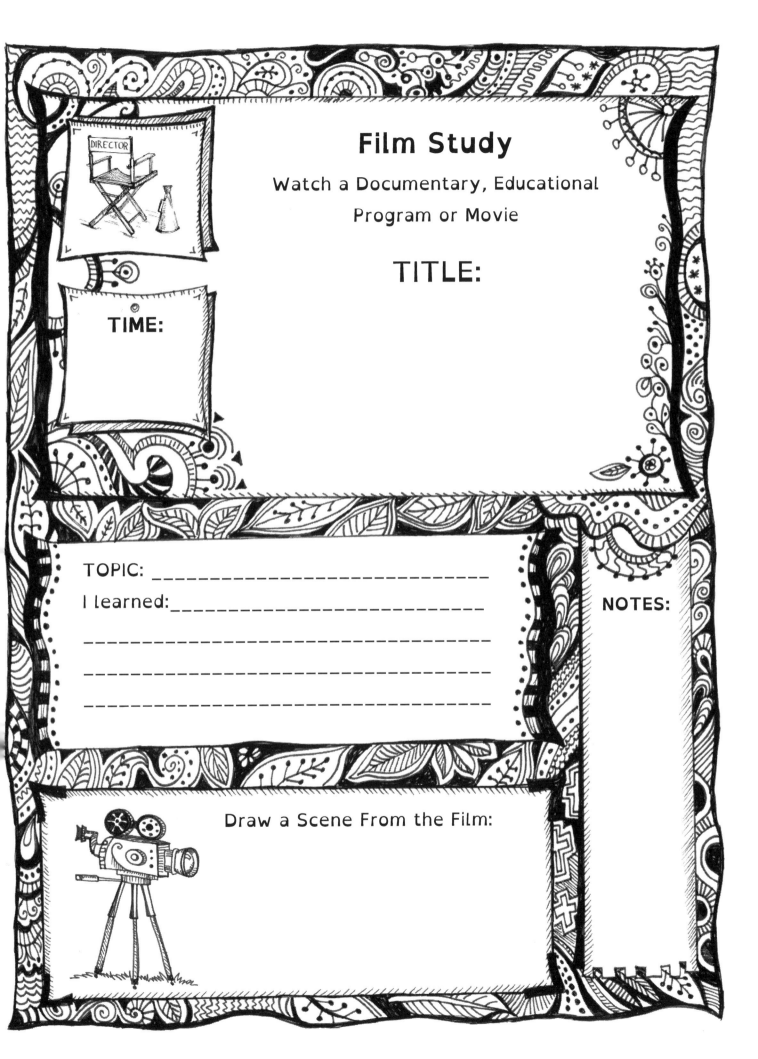

Film Study

Watch a Documentary, Educational
Program or Movie

TITLE:

TIME:

TOPIC: _____

I learned:_____

_____

_____

_____

NOTES:

Draw a Scene From the Film:

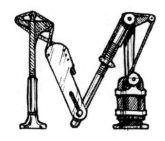

Math Practice

Watch a math tutorial or open up a math book.
You can practice math problems here.

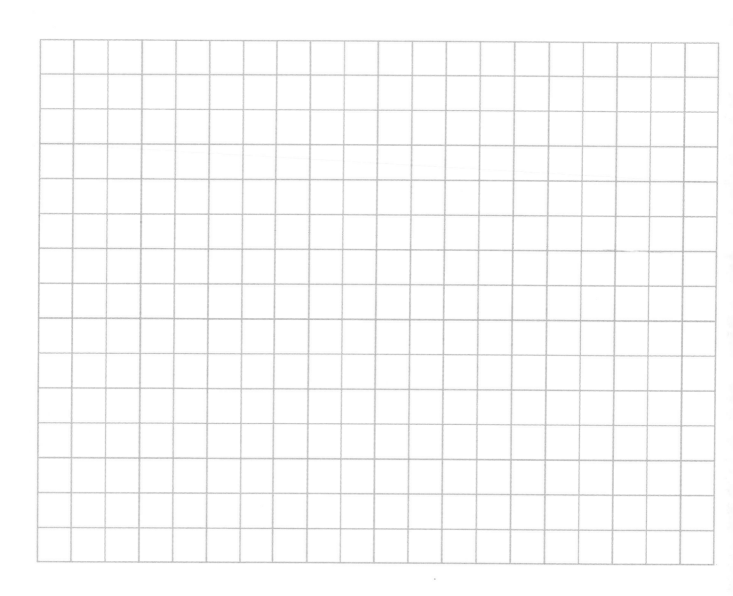

Listening Time

Listen to an audio book or classical music or
ask someone to read a story to you while
you color and draw on the next page.

What are you listening to?

_____

Circle
Today's Date

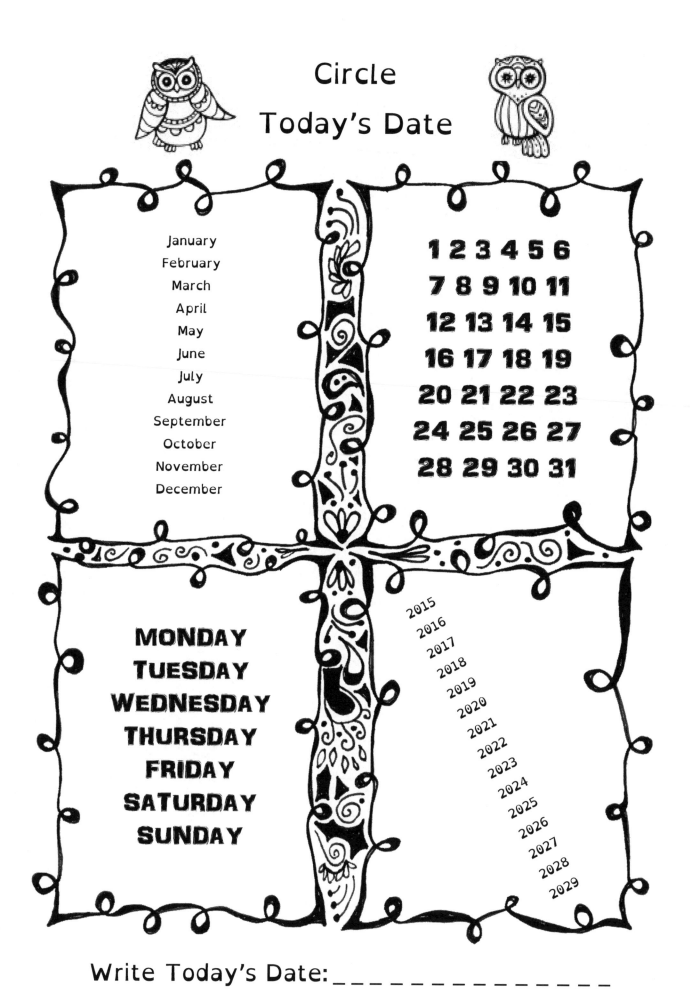

January
February
March
April
May
June
July
August
September
October
November
December

1 2 3 4 5 6
7 8 9 10 11
12 13 14 15
16 17 18 19
20 21 22 23
24 25 26 27
28 29 30 31

**MONDAY
TUESDAY
WEDNESDAY
THURSDAY
FRIDAY
SATURDAY
SUNDAY**

2015
2016
2017
2018
2019
2020
2021
2022
2023
2024
2025
2026
2027
2028
2029

Write Today's Date:_____

My Thinking Page

This is where you write down your ideas, goals,
and plans - with a thankful heart!

Ideas

Goals

I Am Thankful For...

Checklist

Creative Writing

Draw a picture below.

Write a poem or short story about it.

TITLE: _____

_____

_____

_____

_____

_____

_____

_____

_____

_____

_____

_____

_____

_____

_____

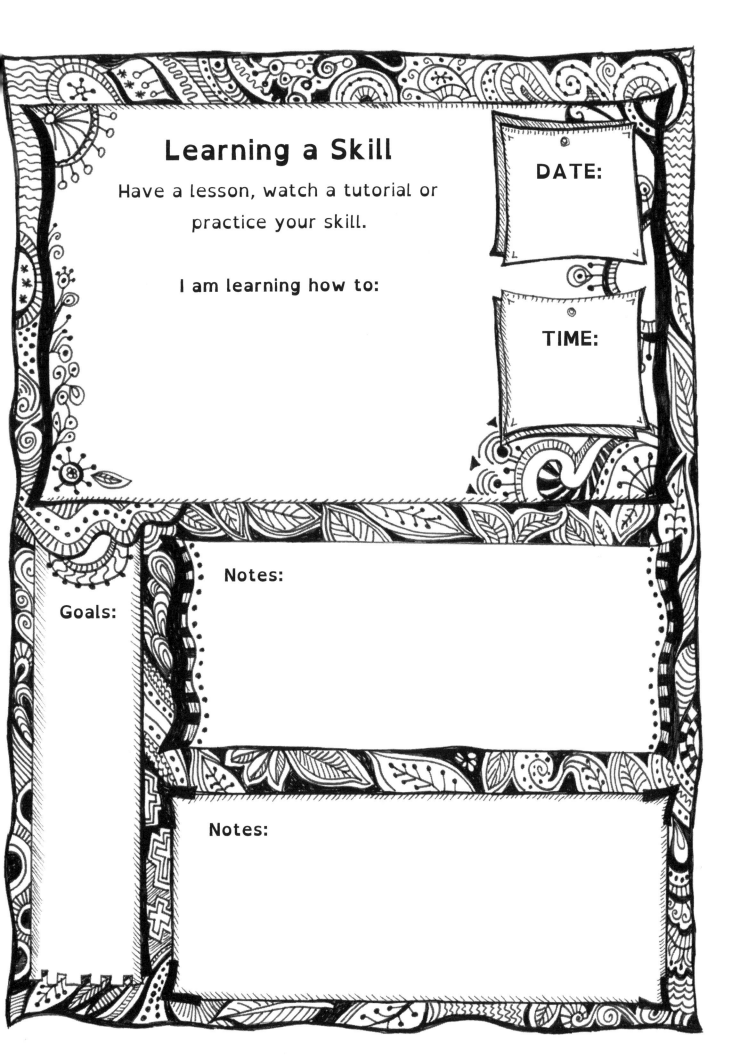

Learning a Skill

Have a lesson, watch a tutorial or practice your skill.

I am learning how to:

DATE:

TIME:

Goals:

Notes:

Notes:

Nature Study

Go outside and make a realistic
drawing of something you find in nature.

Reading Time - 1 Hour

Choose Four Books - Read from each book for 15 minutes.

Copy a sentence or picture from each book here:

Circle
Today's Date

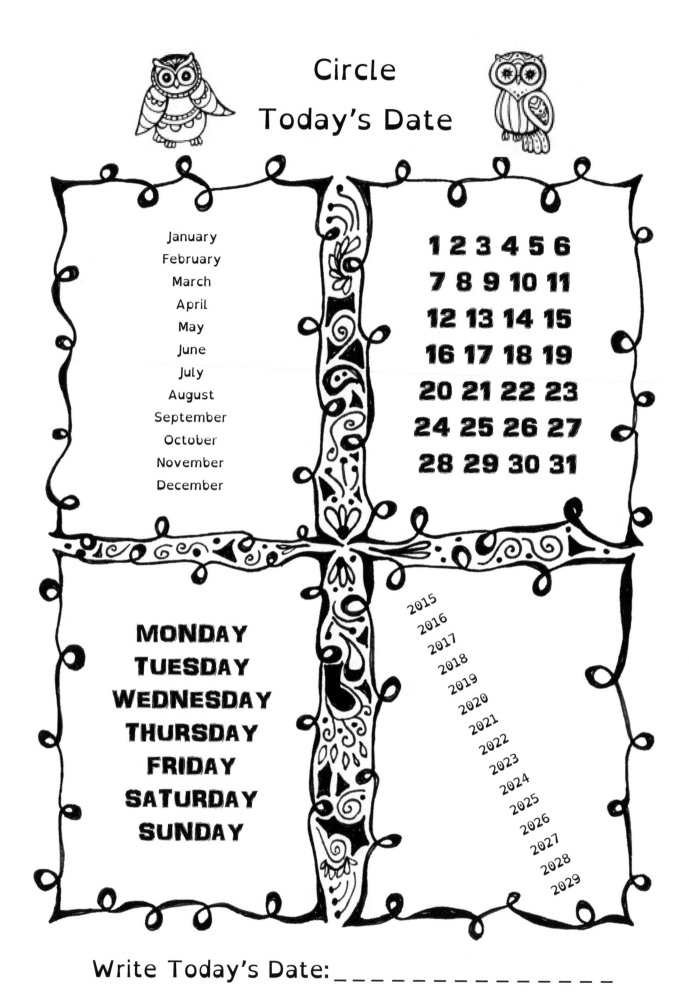

January
February
March
April
May
June
July
August
September
October
November
December

1 2 3 4 5 6
7 8 9 10 11
12 13 14 15
16 17 18 19
20 21 22 23
24 25 26 27
28 29 30 31

MONDAY
TUESDAY
WEDNESDAY
THURSDAY
FRIDAY
SATURDAY
SUNDAY

2015
2016
2017
2018
2019
2020
2021
2022
2023
2024
2025
2026
2027
2028
2029

Write Today's Date: _ _ _ _ _ _ _ _ _ _ _ _ _ _ _ _

My Illustrated TO-DO List

Film Study

Watch a Documentary, Educational Program or Movie

TITLE:

TIME:

TOPIC: _____

I learned: _____

_____

_____

_____

NOTES:

Draw a Scene From the Film:

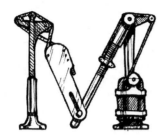

Math Practice

Watch a math tutorial or open up a math book.
You can practice math problems here.

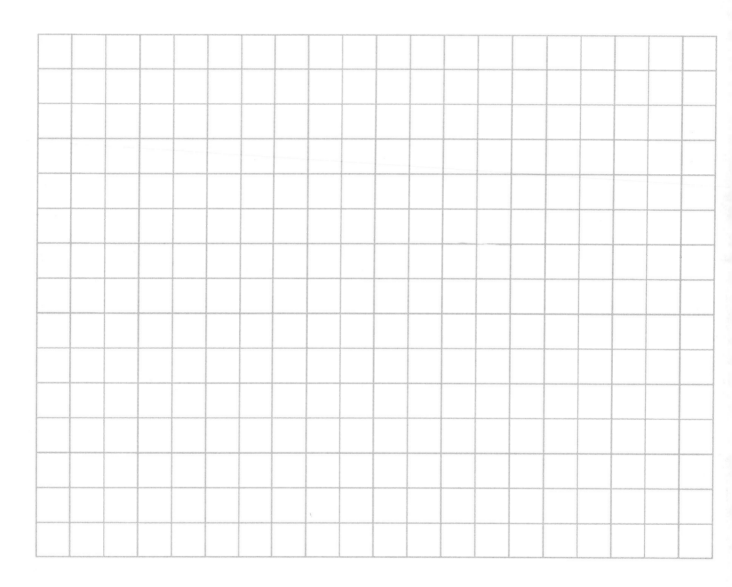

Copywork

Find an interesting paragraph in one of your books and copy it. Be diligent to make your writing look exactly like it does in the book.

TITLE:_____ **Page Number:_____**

_____

_____

_____

_____

_____

_____

_____

_____

_____

_____

_____

_____

_____

_____

Sketch a Picture

Look through your library books and find something to draw.

Circle
Today's Date

January
February
March
April
May
June
July
August
September
October
November
December

1 2 3 4 5 6
7 8 9 10 11
12 13 14 15
16 17 18 19
20 21 22 23
24 25 26 27
28 29 30 31

MONDAY
TUESDAY
WEDNESDAY
THURSDAY
FRIDAY
SATURDAY
SUNDAY

2015
2016
2017
2018
2019
2020
2021
2022
2023
2024
2025
2026
2027
2028
2029

Write Today's Date: _ _ _ _ _ _ _ _ _ _ _ _ _ _ _ _

My Thinking Page

This is where you write down your ideas, goals,
and plans - with a thankful heart!

Ideas

Goals

I Am Thankful For...

Checklist

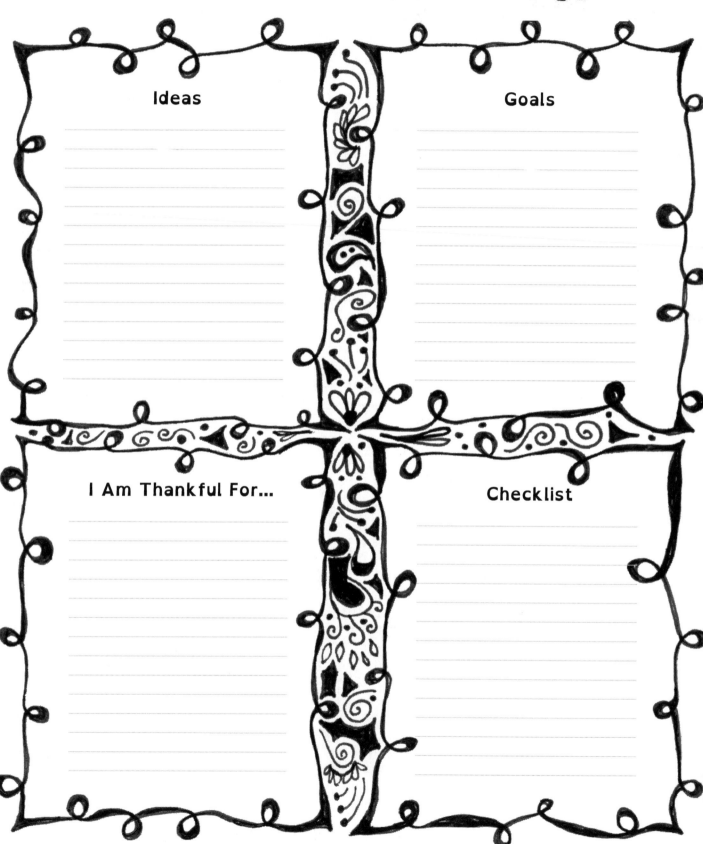

Creative Writing

Draw a picture below.

Write a poem or short story about it.

TITLE: _____

_____

_____

_____

_____

_____

_____

_____

_____

_____

_____

_____

_____

_____

Nature Study

Go outside and make a realistic
drawing of something you find in nature.

Reading Time - 1 Hour

Choose Four Books - Read from each book for 15 minutes.

Copy a sentence or picture from each book here:

Circle
Today's Date

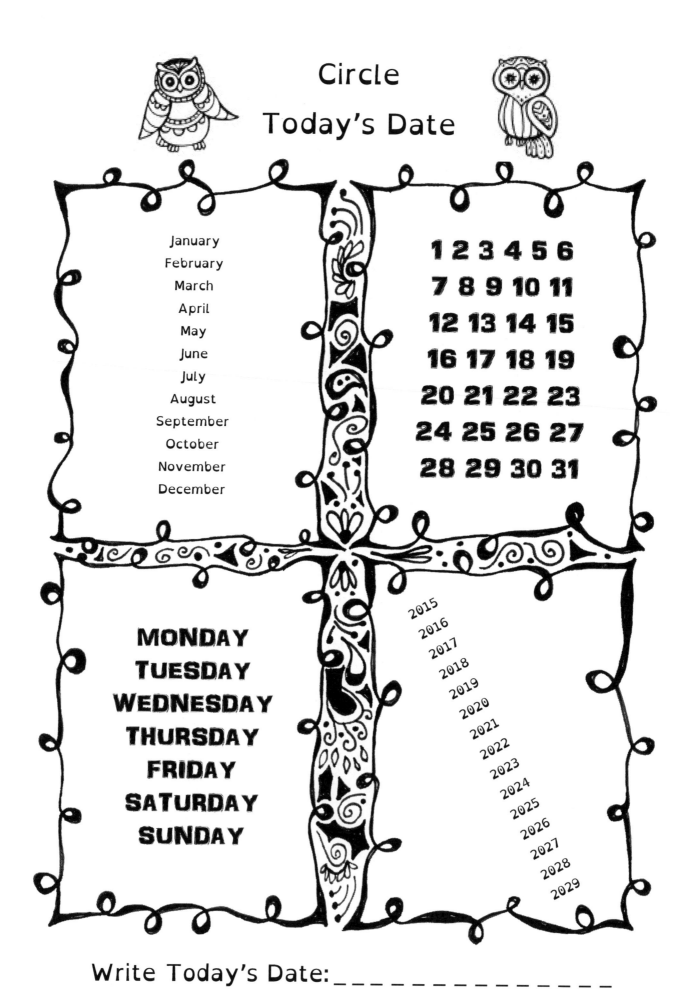

January
February
March
April
May
June
July
August
September
October
November
December

1 2 3 4 5 6
7 8 9 10 11
12 13 14 15
16 17 18 19
20 21 22 23
24 25 26 27
28 29 30 31

MONDAY
TUESDAY
WEDNESDAY
THURSDAY
FRIDAY
SATURDAY
SUNDAY

2015
2016
2017
2018
2019
2020
2021
2022
2023
2024
2025
2026
2027
2028
2029

Write Today's Date: _ _ _ _ _ _ _ _ _ _ _ _ _ _ _ _ _ _

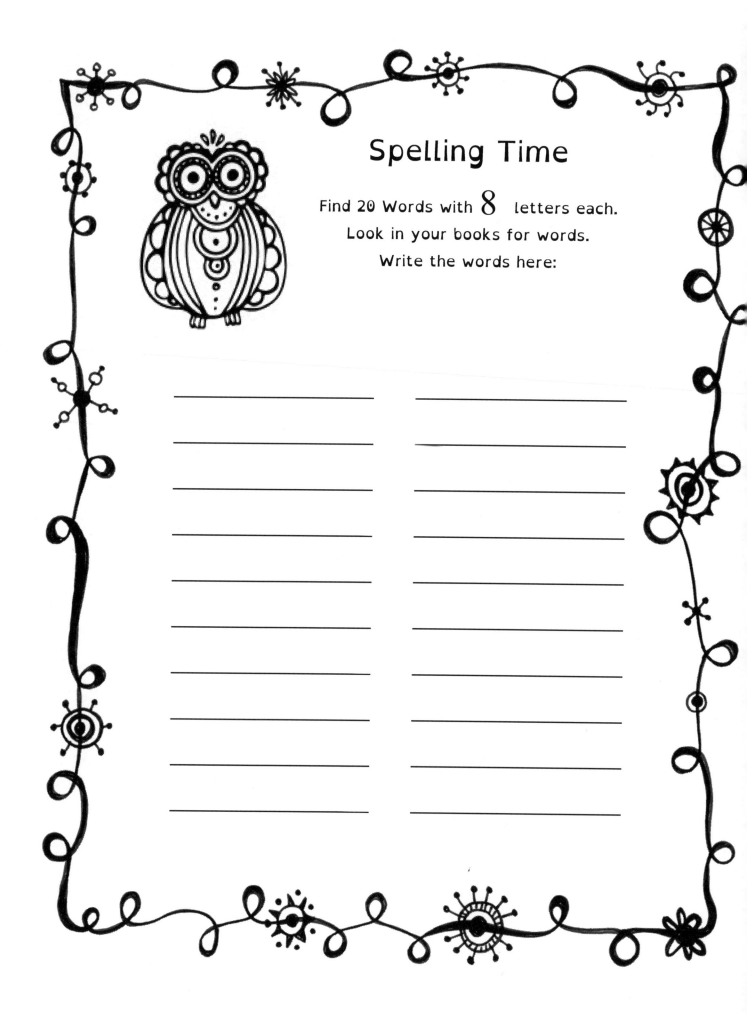

Spelling Time

Find 20 Words with **8** letters each.

Look in your books for words.

Write the words here:

Film Study

Watch a Documentary, Educational Program or Movie

TITLE:

TIME:

TOPIC: _____

I learned: _____

_____

_____

_____

NOTES:

Draw a Scene From the Film:

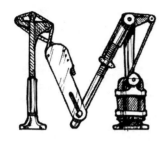

Math Practice

Watch a math tutorial or open up a math book.

You can practice math problems here.

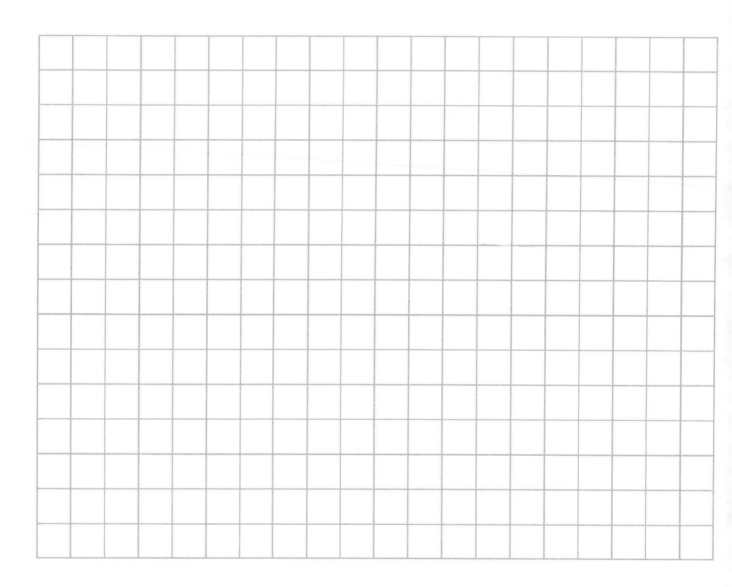

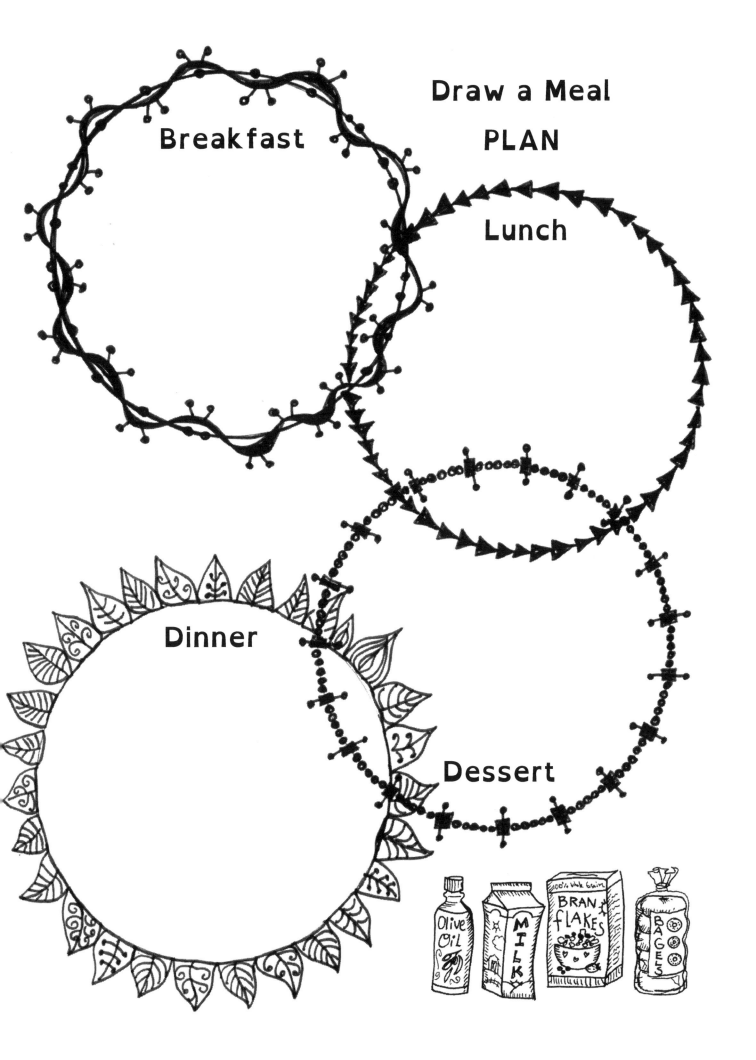

Breakfast

Draw a Meal
PLAN

Lunch

Dinner

Dessert

Art & Creativity Time

Copywork

Find an interesting paragraph in one of your books and copy it. Be diligent to make your writing look exactly like it does in the book.

TITLE:_____ **Page Number:**_____

_____

_____

_____

_____

_____

_____

_____

_____

_____

_____

_____

_____

_____

_____

_____

_____

Circle
Today's Date

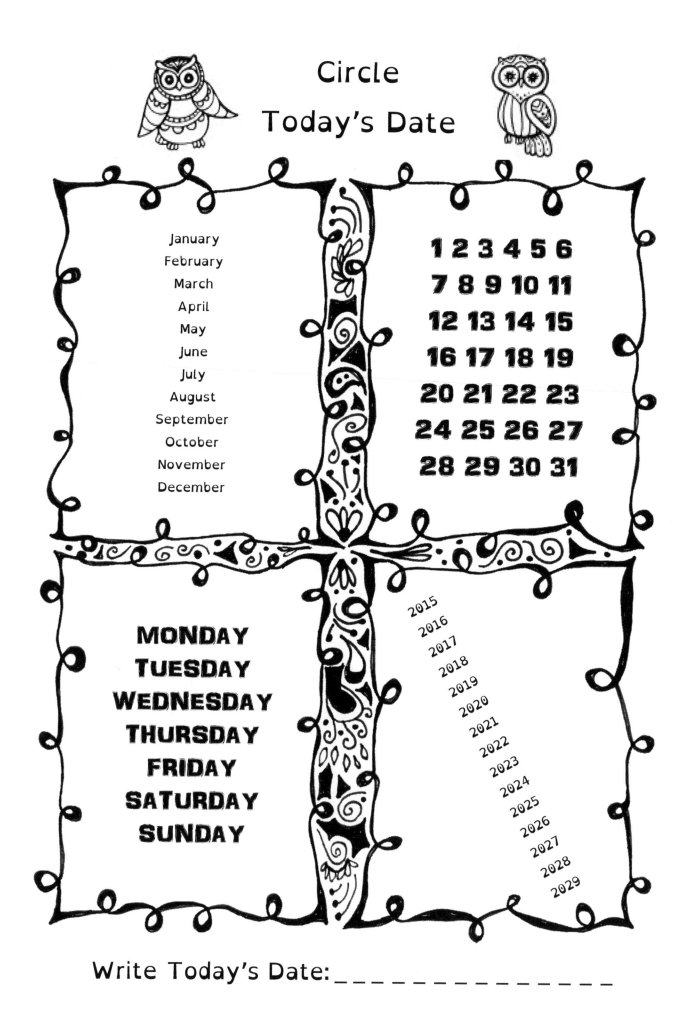

January
February
March
April
May
June
July
August
September
October
November
December

1 2 3 4 5 6
7 8 9 10 11
12 13 14 15
16 17 18 19
20 21 22 23
24 25 26 27
28 29 30 31

MONDAY
TUESDAY
WEDNESDAY
THURSDAY
FRIDAY
SATURDAY
SUNDAY

2015
2016
2017
2018
2019
2020
2021
2022
2023
2024
2025
2026
2027
2028
2029

Write Today's Date: _ _ _ _ _ _ _ _ _ _ _ _ _ _ _

My Thinking Page

This is where you write down your ideas, goals,
and plans - with a thankful heart!

Ideas

Goals

I Am Thankful For...

Checklist

Creative Writing

Draw a picture below.
Write a poem or short story about it.

TITLE: _____

_____
_____
_____
_____
_____
_____
_____
_____
_____
_____
_____
_____
_____
_____

Nature Study

Go outside and make a realistic
drawing of something you find in nature.

Reading Time - 1 Hour

Choose Four Books - Read from each book for 15 minutes.

Copy a sentence or picture from each book here:

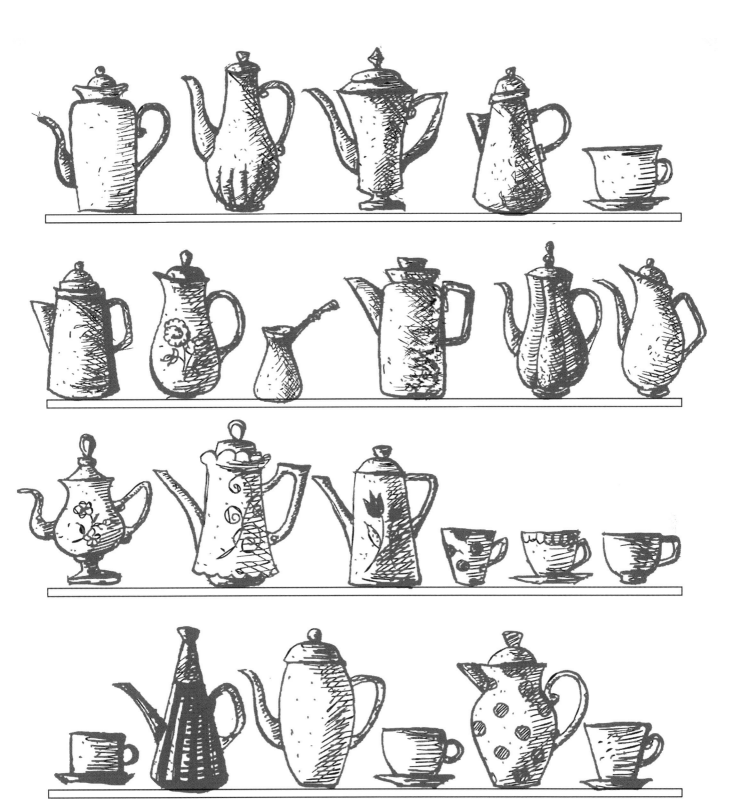

Circle
Today's Date

January
February
March
April
May
June
July
August
September
October
November
December

1 2 3 4 5 6
7 8 9 10 11
12 13 14 15
16 17 18 19
20 21 22 23
24 25 26 27
28 29 30 31

MONDAY
TUESDAY
WEDNESDAY
THURSDAY
FRIDAY
SATURDAY
SUNDAY

2015
2016
2017
2018
2019
2020
2021
2022
2023
2024
2025
2026
2027
2028
2029

Write Today's Date: _ _ _ _ _ _ _ _ _ _ _ _ _ _ _ _ _

Spelling Time

Find 20 Words with 8 letters each.

Look in your books for words.

Write the words here:

Film Study

Watch a Documentary, Educational Program or Movie

TITLE:

TIME:

TOPIC: _____

I learned:_____

_____

_____

_____

NOTES:

Draw a Scene From the Film:

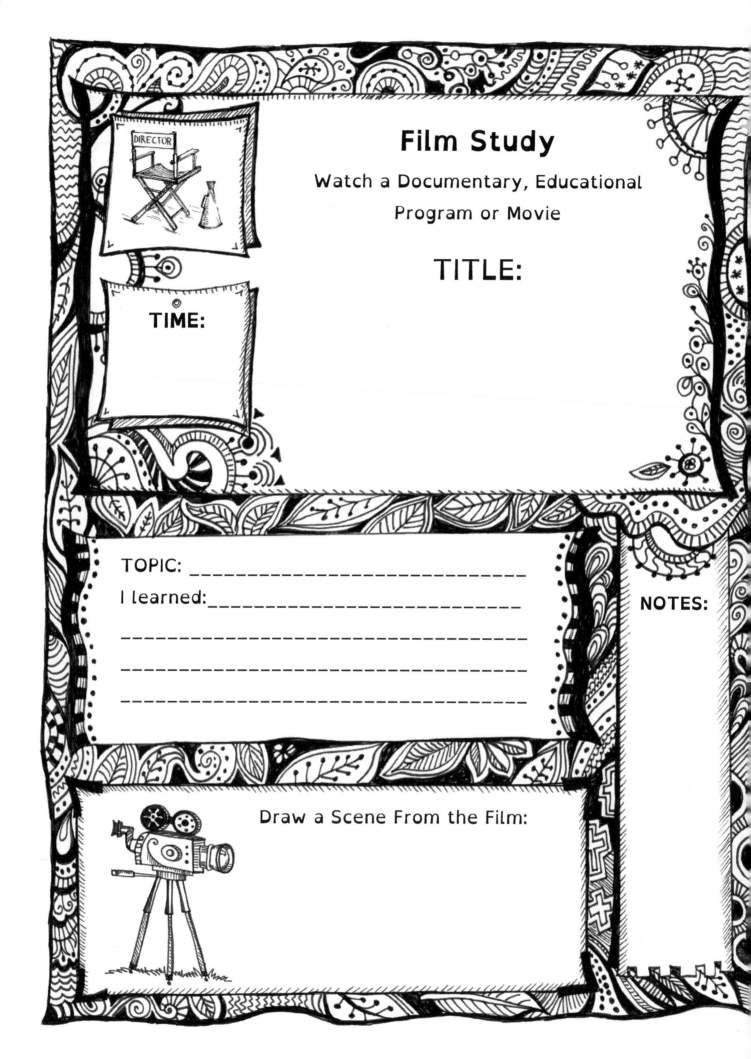

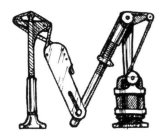

Math Practice

Watch a math tutorial or open up a math book.

You can practice math problems here.

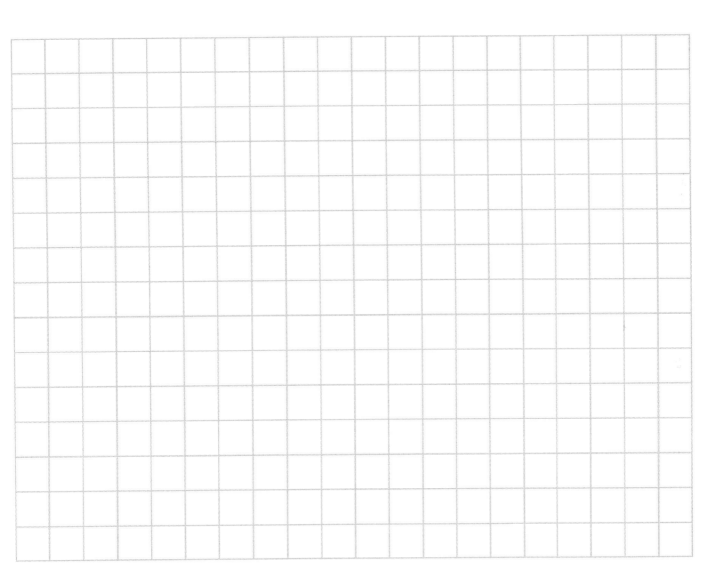

Copywork

Find an interesting paragraph in one of your books and copy it. Be diligent to make your writing look exactly like it does in the book.

TITLE:_____ **Page Number:**_____

_____

_____

_____

_____

_____

_____

_____

_____

_____

_____

_____

_____

_____

_____

_____

Sketch a Picture

Look through your library books and find something to draw.

Circle
Today's Date

January
February
March
April
May
June
July
August
September
October
November
December

1 2 3 4 5 6
7 8 9 10 11
12 13 14 15
16 17 18 19
20 21 22 23
24 25 26 27
28 29 30 31

MONDAY
TUESDAY
WEDNESDAY
THURSDAY
FRIDAY
SATURDAY
SUNDAY

2015
2016
2017
2018
2019
2020
2021
2022
2023
2024
2025
2026
2027
2028
2029

Write Today's Date: _____

My Thinking Page

This is where you write down your ideas, goals,
and plans - with a thankful heart!

Ideas

Goals

I Am Thankful For...

Checklist

Creative Writing

Draw a picture below.

Write a poem or short story about it.

TITLE: _____

_____
_____
_____
_____
_____
_____
_____
_____
_____
_____
_____
_____
_____

Nature Study

Go outside and make a realistic
drawing of something you find in nature.

Reading Time - 1 Hour

Choose Four Books - Read from each book for 15 minutes.

Copy a sentence or picture from each book here:

Learning a Skill

Have a lesson, watch a tutorial or practice your skill.

I am learning how to:

DATE:

TIME:

Goals:

Notes:

Notes:

Circle
Today's Date

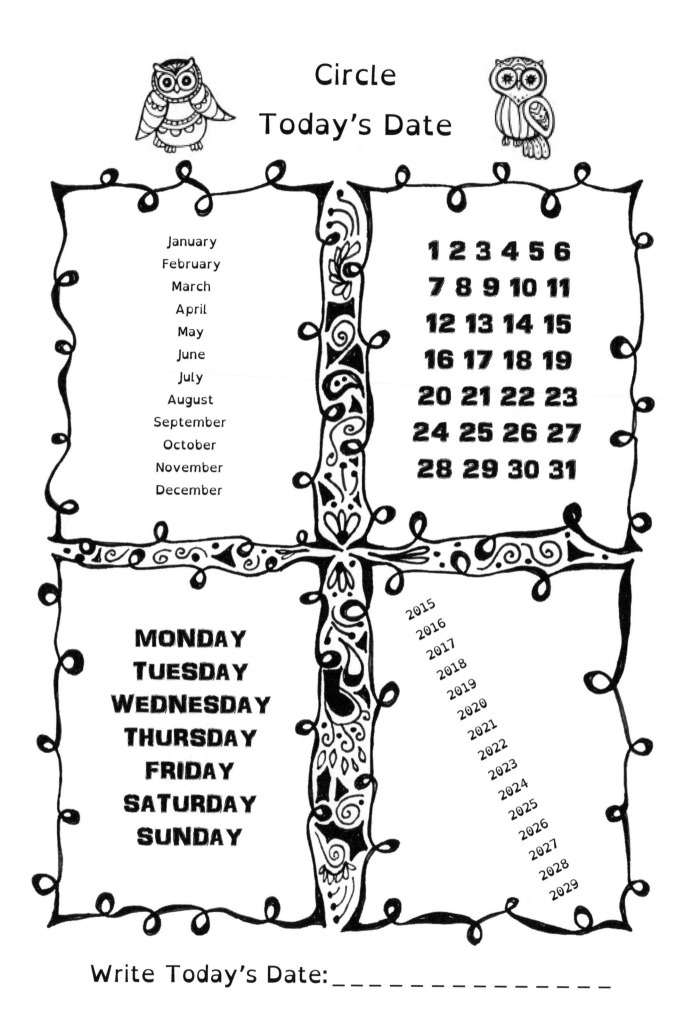

January
February
March
April
May
June
July
August
September
October
November
December

1 2 3 4 5 6
7 8 9 10 11
12 13 14 15
16 17 18 19
20 21 22 23
24 25 26 27
28 29 30 31

MONDAY
TUESDAY
WEDNESDAY
THURSDAY
FRIDAY
SATURDAY
SUNDAY

2015
2016
2017
2018
2019
2020
2021
2022
2023
2024
2025
2026
2027
2028
2029

Write Today's Date: _____

Spelling Time

Find 20 Words with 7 letters each.
Look in your books for words.
Write the words here:

_____   _____

_____   _____

_____   _____

_____   _____

_____   _____

_____   _____

_____   _____

_____   _____

_____   _____

_____   _____

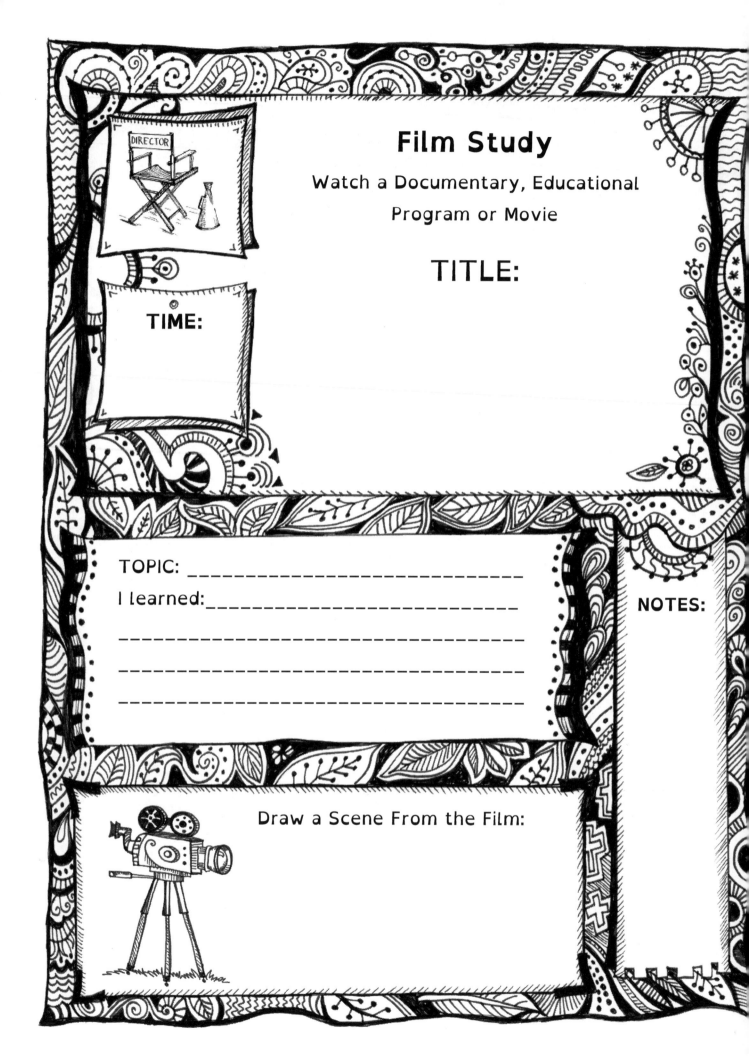

Film Study

Watch a Documentary, Educational Program or Movie

TITLE:

TIME:

TOPIC: _____

I learned:_____

_____

_____

_____

NOTES:

Draw a Scene From the Film:

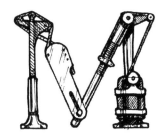

Math Practice

Watch a math tutorial or open up a math book.

You can practice math problems here.

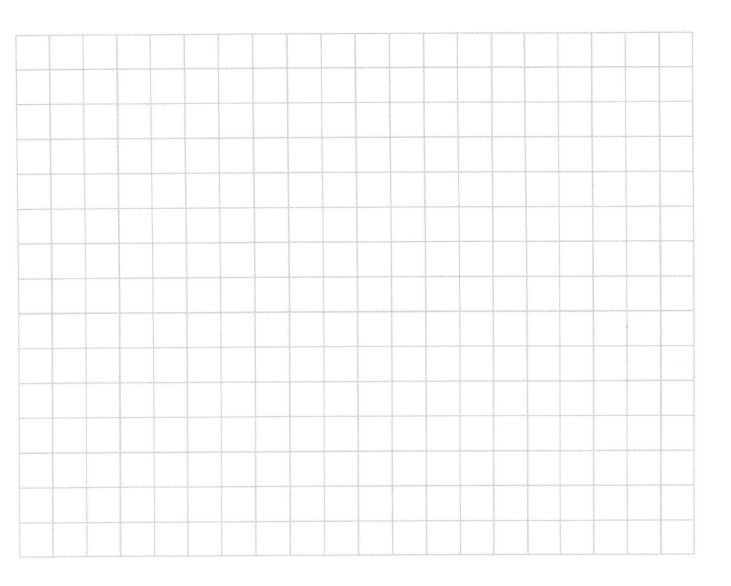

Copywork

Find an interesting paragraph in one of your books and copy it. Be diligent to make your writing look exactly like it does in the book.

TITLE:_____ **Page Number:**_____

_____

_____

_____

_____

_____

_____

_____

_____

_____

_____

_____

_____

_____

_____

Circle
Today's Date

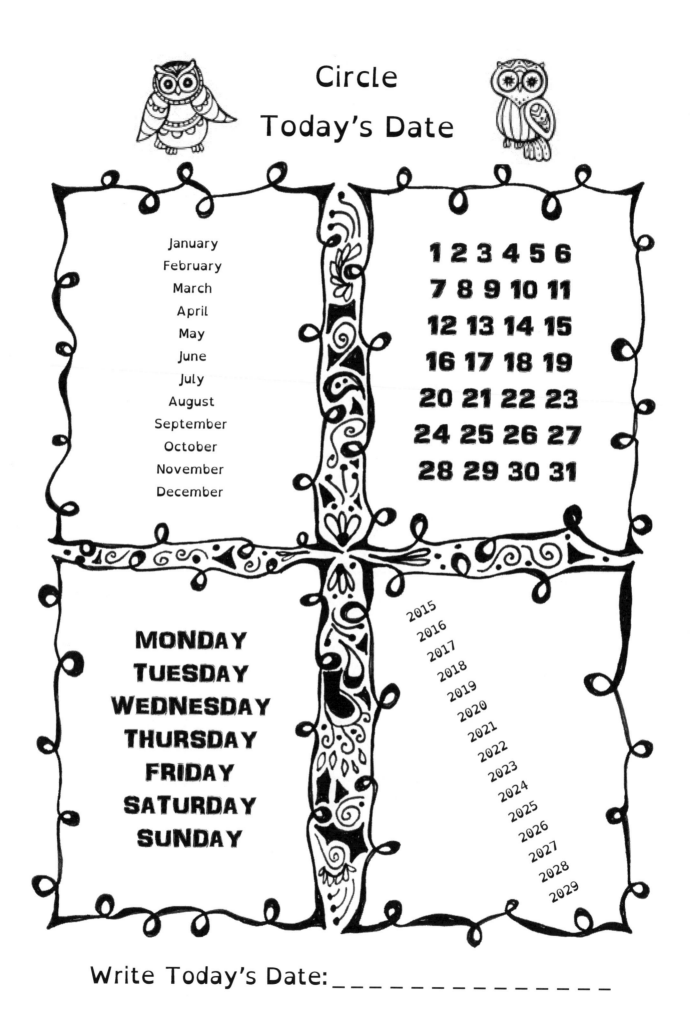

January
February
March
April
May
June
July
August
September
October
November
December

1 2 3 4 5 6
7 8 9 10 11
12 13 14 15
16 17 18 19
20 21 22 23
24 25 26 27
28 29 30 31

MONDAY
TUESDAY
WEDNESDAY
THURSDAY
FRIDAY
SATURDAY
SUNDAY

2015
2016
2017
2018
2019
2020
2021
2022
2023
2024
2025
2026
2027
2028
2029

Write Today's Date: _ _ _ _ _ _ _ _ _ _ _ _ _ _ _ _ _

My Thinking Page

This is where you write down your ideas, goals, and plans - with a thankful heart!

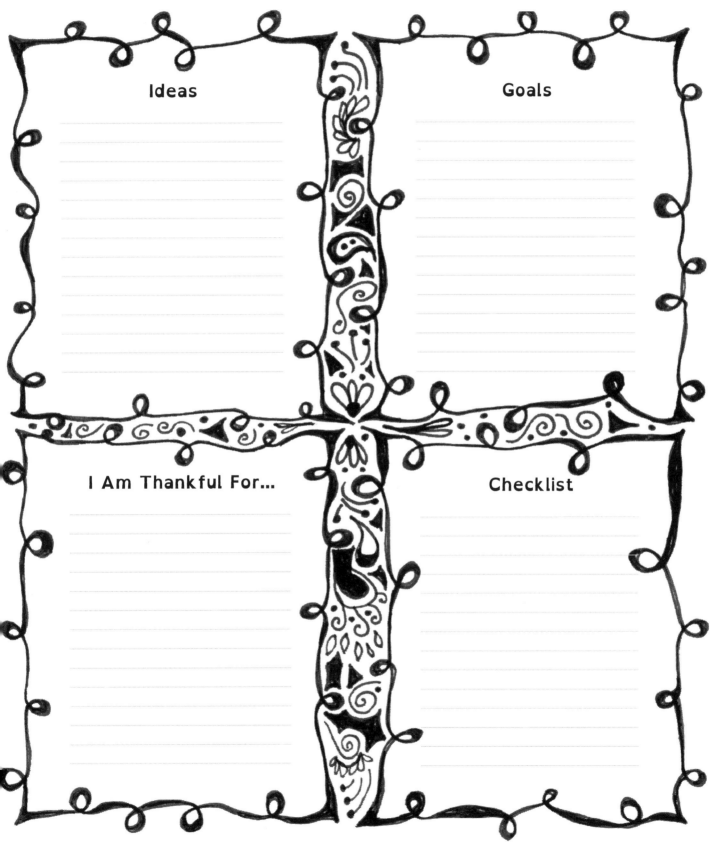

Ideas

Goals

I Am Thankful For...

Checklist

Creative Writing

Draw a picture below.
Write a poem or short story about it.

TITLE: _____

_____
_____
_____
_____
_____
_____
_____
_____
_____
_____
_____
_____

Write & Draw
about something that
really happened.

_____

_____

_____

_____

_____

_____

_____

_____

_____

_____

Circle
Today's Date

January
February
March
April
May
June
July
August
September
October
November
December

1 2 3 4 5 6
7 8 9 10 11
12 13 14 15
16 17 18 19
20 21 22 23
24 25 26 27
28 29 30 31

MONDAY
TUESDAY
WEDNESDAY
THURSDAY
FRIDAY
SATURDAY
SUNDAY

2015
2016
2017
2018
2019
2020
2021
2022
2023
2024
2025
2026
2027
2028
2029

Write Today's Date:_____

Nature Study

Go outside and make a realistic
drawing of something you find in nature.

Reading Time - 1 Hour

Choose Four Books - Read from each book for 15 minutes.

Copy a sentence or picture from each book here:

Spelling Time

Find 20 Words with 6 letters each.

Look in your books for words.

Write the words here:

Film Study

Watch a Documentary, Educational
Program or Movie

TITLE:

TIME:

TOPIC: _____

I learned:_____

_____

_____

_____

NOTES:

Draw a Scene From the Film:

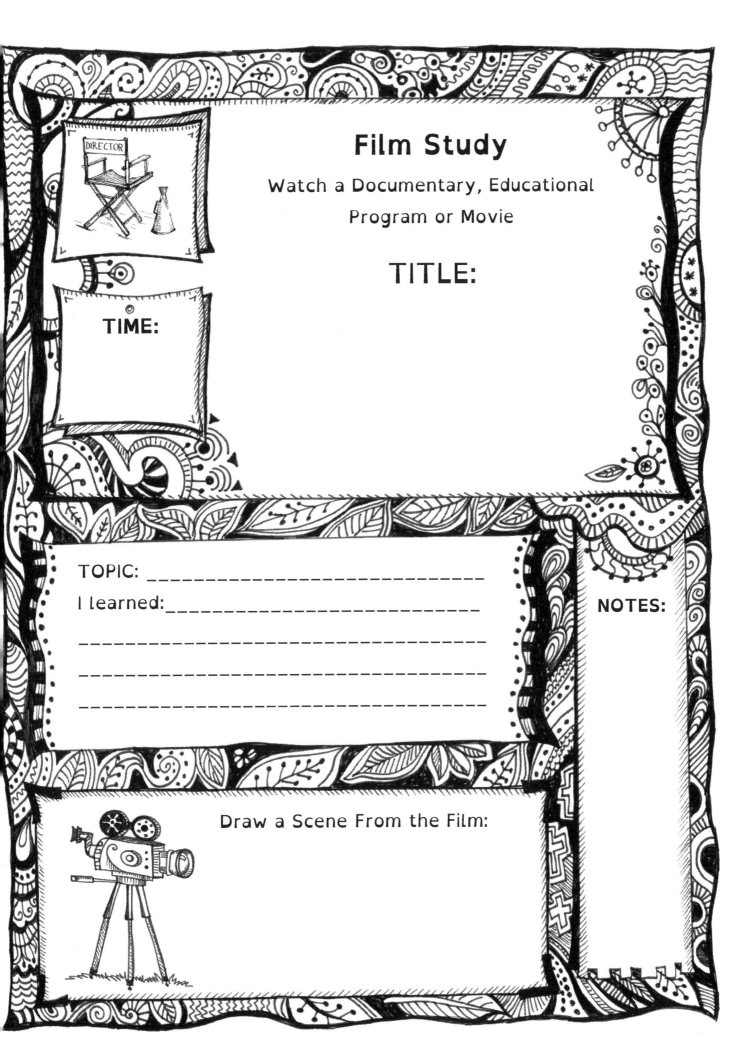

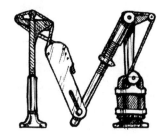

Math Practice

Watch a math tutorial or open up a math book.
You can practice math problems here.

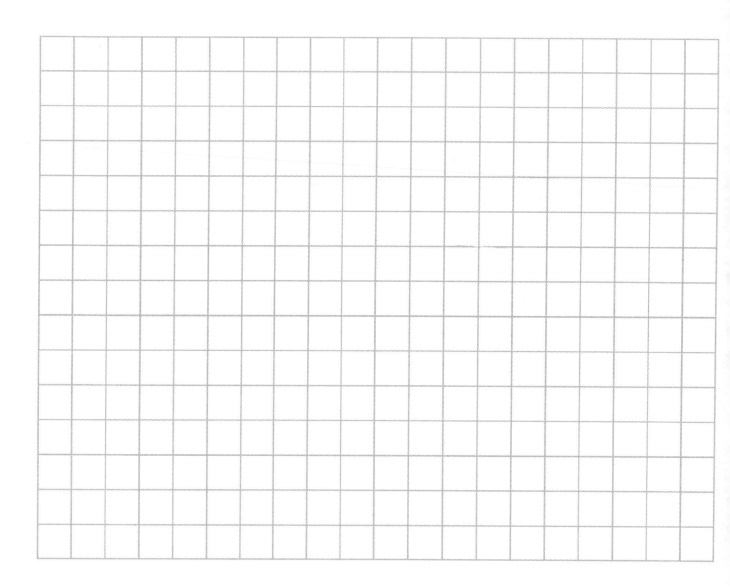

Copywork

Find an interesting paragraph in one of your books and copy it. Be diligent to make your writing look exactly like it does in the book.

TITLE:_____ **Page Number:**_____

_____

_____

_____

_____

_____

_____

_____

_____

_____

_____

_____

_____

_____

_____

Sketch a Picture

Look through your library books and find something to draw.

Circle
Today's Date

January
February
March
April
May
June
July
August
September
October
November
December

1 2 3 4 5 6
7 8 9 10 11
12 13 14 15
16 17 18 19
20 21 22 23
24 25 26 27
28 29 30 31

MONDAY
TUESDAY
WEDNESDAY
THURSDAY
FRIDAY
SATURDAY
SUNDAY

2015
2016
2017
2018
2019
2020
2021
2022
2023
2024
2025
2026
2027
2028
2029

Write Today's Date:_ _ _ _ _ _ _ _ _ _ _ _ _ _ _ _ _

My Thinking Page

This is where you write down your ideas, goals,
and plans - with a thankful heart!

Ideas

Goals

I Am Thankful For...

Checklist

Write & Draw
about something that really happened.

_____

_____

_____

_____

_____

_____

_____

_____

_____

Nature Study

Go outside and make a realistic
drawing of something you find in nature.

Circle Today's Date

January
February
March
April
May
June
July
August
September
October
November
December

1 2 3 4 5 6
7 8 9 10 11
12 13 14 15
16 17 18 19
20 21 22 23
24 25 26 27
28 29 30 31

MONDAY
TUESDAY
WEDNESDAY
THURSDAY
FRIDAY
SATURDAY
SUNDAY

2015
2016
2017
2018
2019
2020
2021
2022
2023
2024
2025
2026
2027
2028
2029

Write Today's Date: _ _ _ _ _ _ _ _ _ _ _ _ _ _ _ _ _

Reading Time - 1 Hour

Choose Four Books - Read from each book for 15 minutes.

Copy a sentence or picture from each book here:

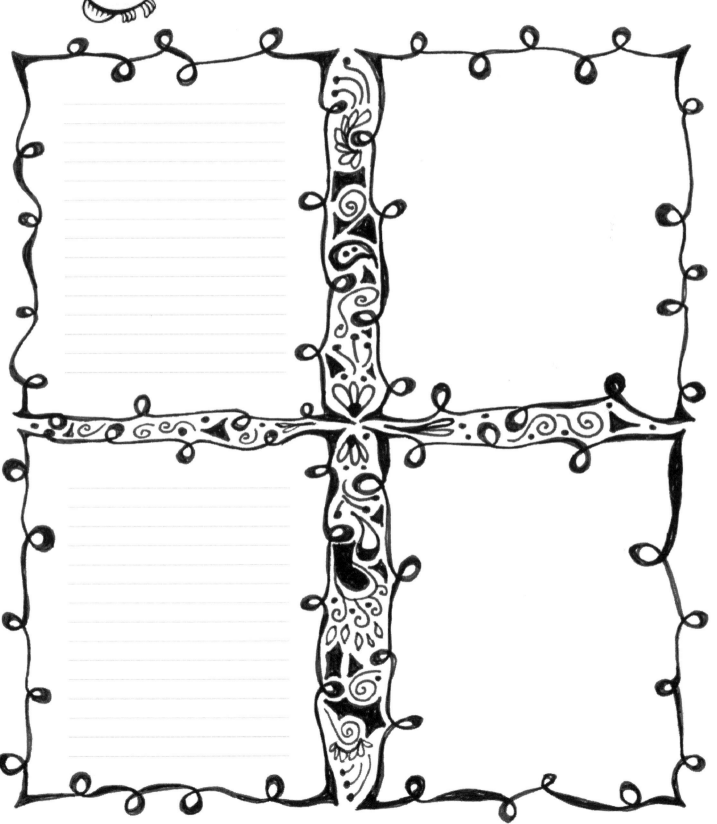

Spelling Time

Find 20 Words with 5 letters each.
Look in your books for words.
Write the words here:

Film Study

Watch a Documentary, Educational Program or Movie

TITLE:

TIME:

TOPIC: _____

I learned:_____

_____

_____

_____

NOTES:

Draw a Scene From the Film:

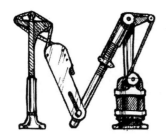

Math Practice

Watch a math tutorial or open up a math book.
You can practice math problems here.

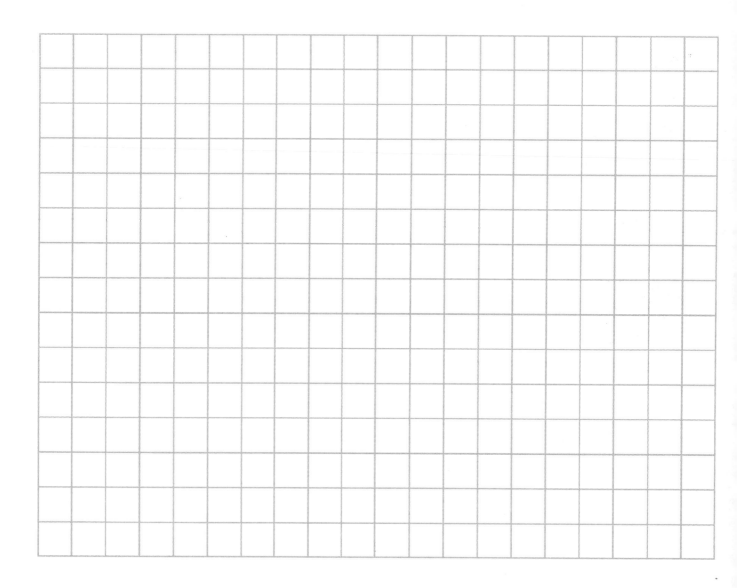

Copywork

Find an interesting paragraph in one of your books and copy it. Be diligent to make your writing look exactly like it does in the book.

TITLE:_____ **Page Number:**_____

_____

_____

_____

_____

_____

_____

_____

_____

_____

_____

_____

_____

_____

_____

Sketch a Picture

Look through your library books and find something to draw.

Circle
Today's Date

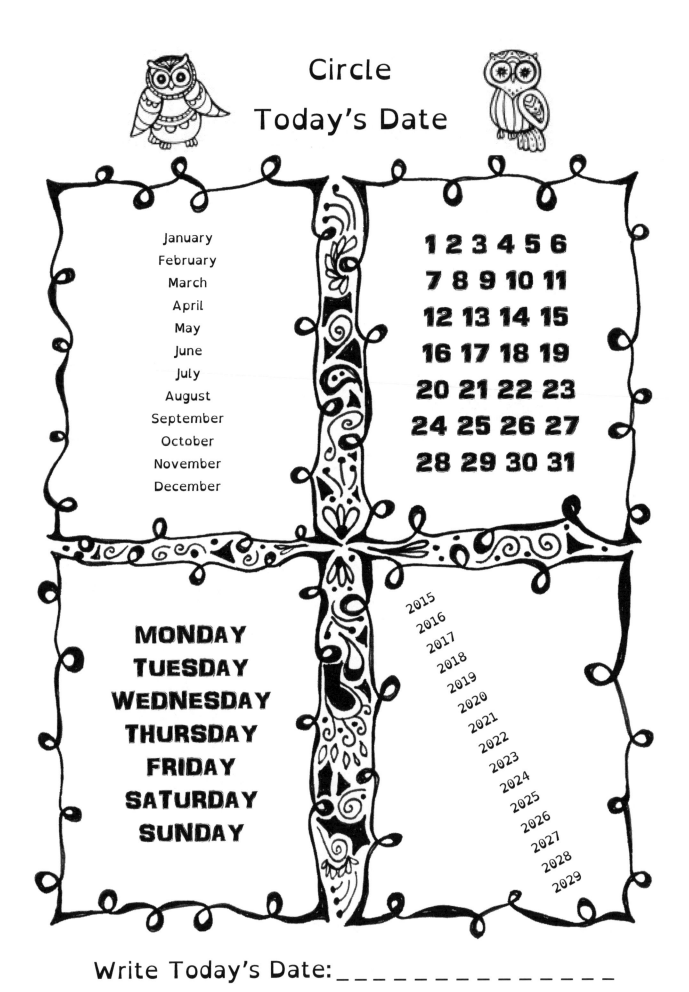

January
February
March
April
May
June
July
August
September
October
November
December

1 2 3 4 5 6
7 8 9 10 11
12 13 14 15
16 17 18 19
20 21 22 23
24 25 26 27
28 29 30 31

MONDAY
TUESDAY
WEDNESDAY
THURSDAY
FRIDAY
SATURDAY
SUNDAY

2015
2016
2017
2018
2019
2020
2021
2022
2023
2024
2025
2026
2027
2028
2029

Write Today's Date: _____

My Thinking Page

This is where you write down your ideas, goals, and plans - with a thankful heart!

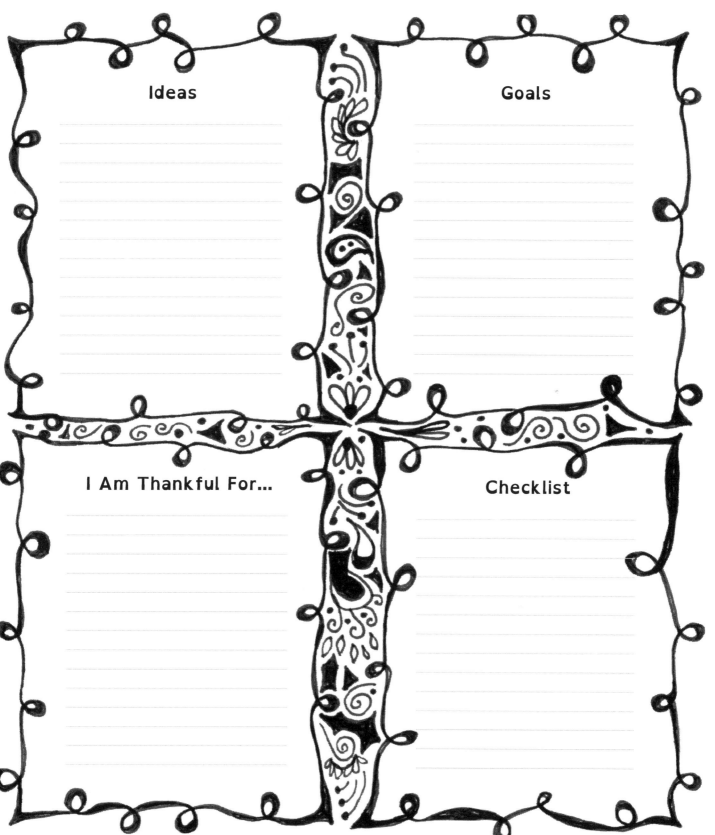

Ideas

Goals

I Am Thankful For...

Checklist

Creative Writing

Draw a picture below.

Write a poem or short story about it.

TITLE: _____

_____

_____

_____

_____

_____

_____

_____

_____

_____

_____

_____

_____

_____

Write & Draw
about something that really happened.

_____
_____
_____
_____
_____
_____
_____
_____
_____

Nature Study

Go outside and make a realistic drawing of something you find in nature.

Circle
Today's Date

January
February
March
April
May
June
July
August
September
October
November
December

1 2 3 4 5 6
7 8 9 10 11
12 13 14 15
16 17 18 19
20 21 22 23
24 25 26 27
28 29 30 31

MONDAY
TUESDAY
WEDNESDAY
THURSDAY
FRIDAY
SATURDAY
SUNDAY

2015
2016
2017
2018
2019
2020
2021
2022
2023
2024
2025
2026
2027
2028
2029

Write Today's Date: _ _ _ _ _ _ _ _ _ _ _ _ _ _ _

Reading Time - 1 Hour

Choose Four Books - Read from each book for 15 minutes.

Copy a sentence or picture from each book here:

Spelling Time

Find 20 Words with 6 letters each.

Look in your books for words.

Write the words here:

Film Study

Watch a Documentary, Educational Program or Movie

TITLE:

TIME:

TOPIC: _____

I learned:_____

_____

_____

_____

NOTES:

Draw a Scene From the Film:

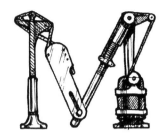

Math Practice

Watch a math tutorial or open up a math book.

You can practice math problems here.

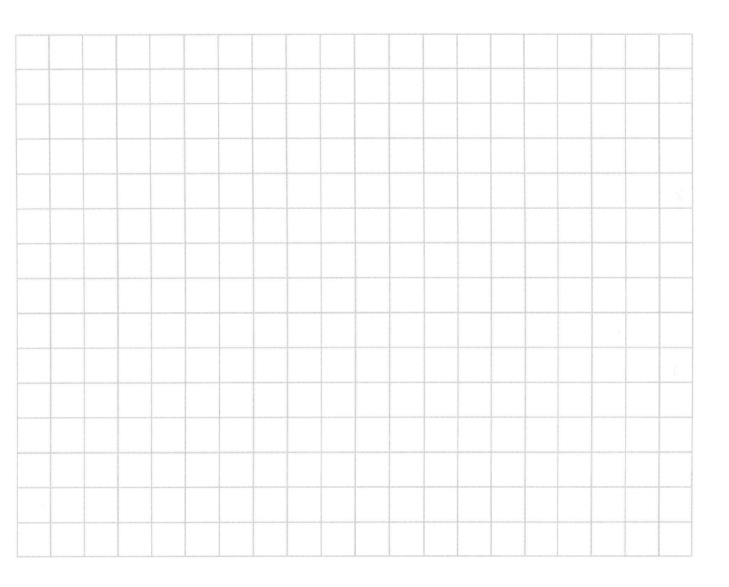

Listening Time

Listen to an audio book or classical music or ask someone to read a story to you while you color and draw on the next page.

What are you listening to?

_____

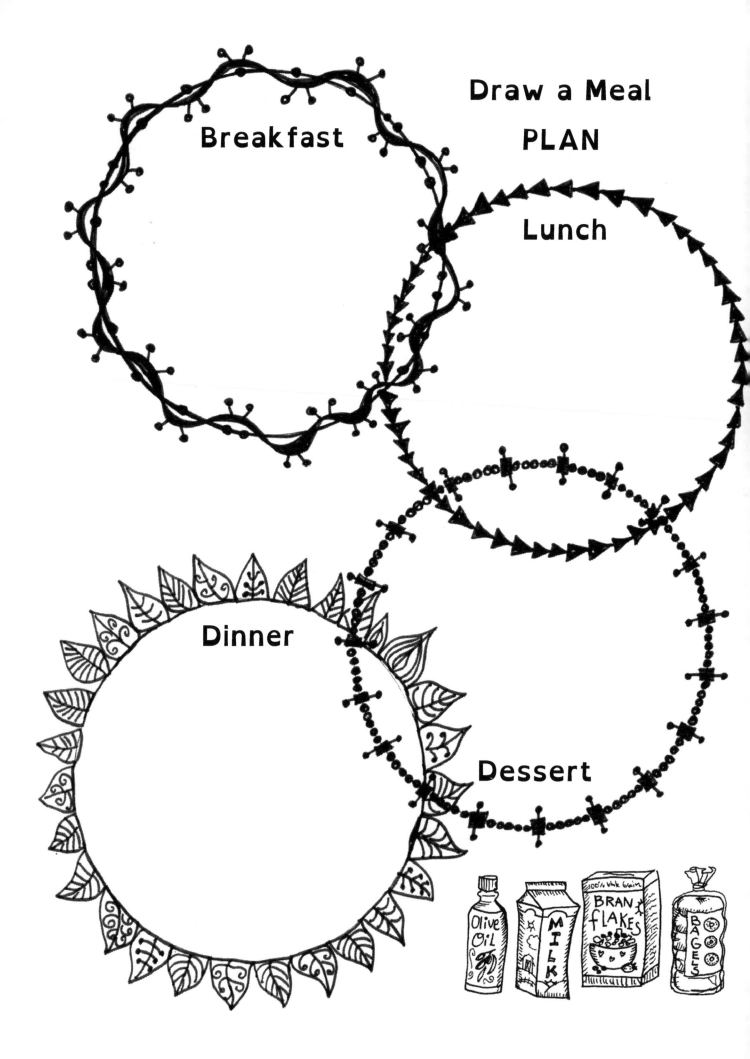

Breakfast

Draw a Meal
PLAN

Lunch

Dinner

Dessert

Circle
Today's Date

January
February
March
April
May
June
July
August
September
October
November
December

1 2 3 4 5 6
7 8 9 10 11
12 13 14 15
16 17 18 19
20 21 22 23
24 25 26 27
28 29 30 31

MONDAY
TUESDAY
WEDNESDAY
THURSDAY
FRIDAY
SATURDAY
SUNDAY

2015
2016
2017
2018
2019
2020
2021
2022
2023
2024
2025
2026
2027
2028
2029

Write Today's Date: _ _ _ _ _ _ _ _ _ _ _ _ _ _ _ _ _ _ _

My Thinking Page

This is where you write down your ideas, goals,
and plans - with a thankful heart!

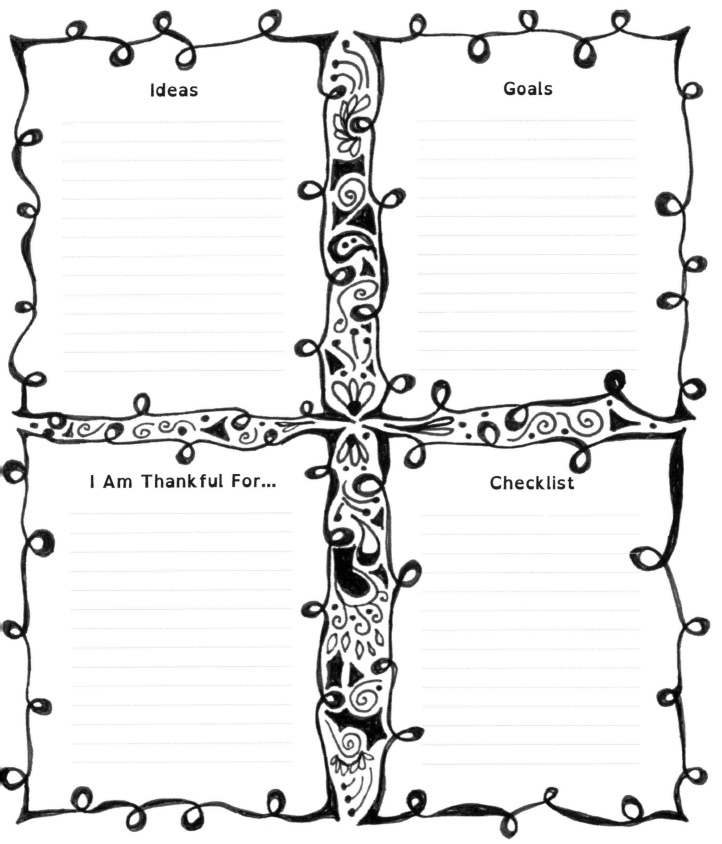

Ideas

Goals

I Am Thankful For...

Checklist

Creative Writing

Draw a picture below.

Write a poem or short story about it.

TITLE: _____

_____

_____

_____

_____

_____

_____

_____

_____

_____

_____

_____

_____

_____

Nature Study

Go outside and make a realistic
drawing of something you find in nature.

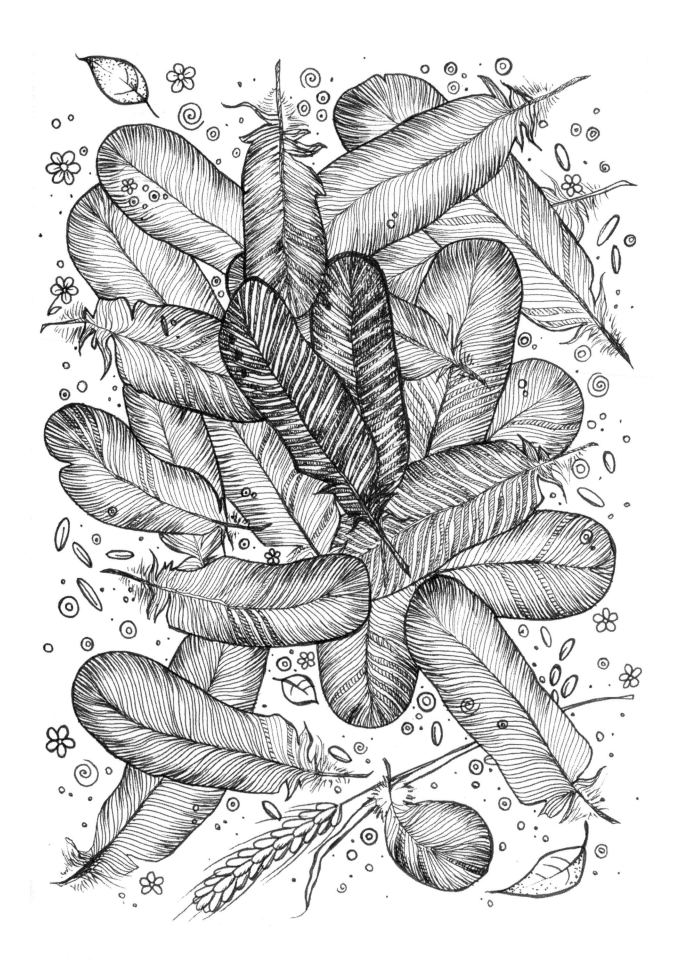

Reading Time - 1 Hour

Choose Four Books - Read from each book for 15 minutes.

Copy a sentence or picture from each book here:

Circle
Today's Date

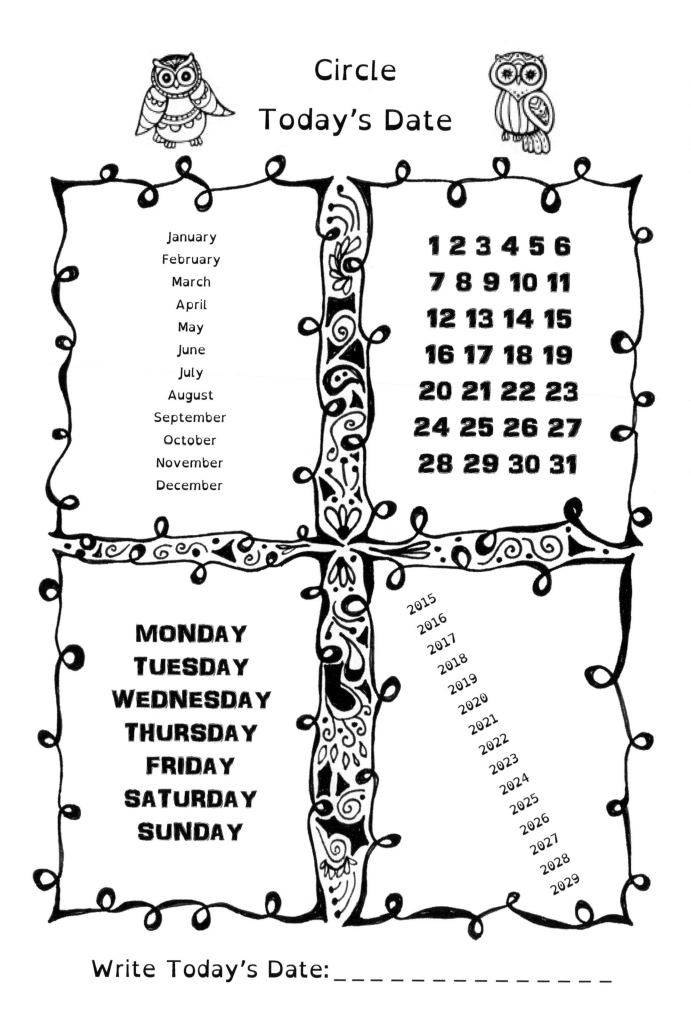

January
February
March
April
May
June
July
August
September
October
November
December

1 2 3 4 5 6
7 8 9 10 11
12 13 14 15
16 17 18 19
20 21 22 23
24 25 26 27
28 29 30 31

MONDAY
TUESDAY
WEDNESDAY
THURSDAY
FRIDAY
SATURDAY
SUNDAY

2015
2016
2017
2018
2019
2020
2021
2022
2023
2024
2025
2026
2027
2028
2029

Write Today's Date: _____

Spelling Time

Find 20 Words with 7 letters each.

Look in your books for words.

Write the words here:

Film Study

Watch a Documentary, Educational Program or Movie

TITLE:

TIME:

TOPIC: _____

I learned: _____

_____

_____

_____

NOTES:

Draw a Scene From the Film:

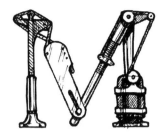

Math Practice

Watch a math tutorial or open up a math book.
You can practice math problems here.

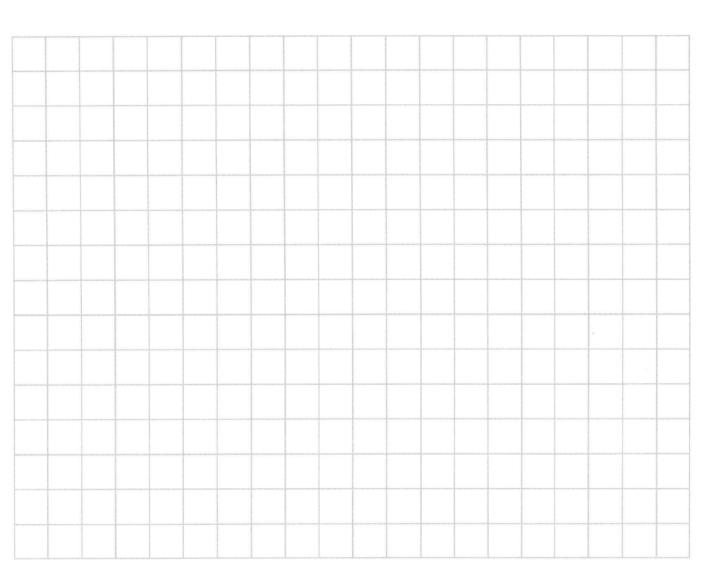

Copywork

Find an interesting paragraph in one of your books and copy it. Be diligent to make your writing look exactly like it does in the book.

TITLE:_____ **Page Number:_____**

_____

_____

_____

_____

_____

_____

_____

_____

_____

_____

_____

_____

_____

_____

_____

Circle
Today's Date

January
February
March
April
May
June
July
August
September
October
November
December

1 2 3 4 5 6
7 8 9 10 11
12 13 14 15
16 17 18 19
20 21 22 23
24 25 26 27
28 29 30 31

MONDAY
TUESDAY
WEDNESDAY
THURSDAY
FRIDAY
SATURDAY
SUNDAY

2015
2016
2017
2018
2019
2020
2021
2022
2023
2024
2025
2026
2027
2028
2029

Write Today's Date:_ _ _ _ _ _ _ _ _ _ _ _ _ _

My Thinking Page

This is where you write down your ideas, goals,
and plans - with a thankful heart!

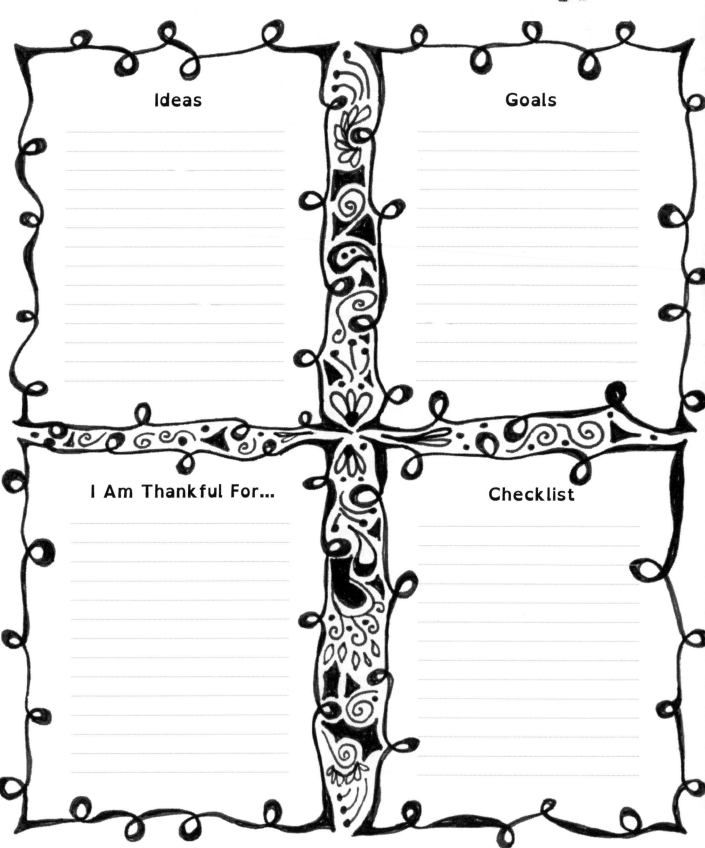

Ideas

Goals

I Am Thankful For...

Checklist

Sketch a Picture

Look through your library books and find something to draw.

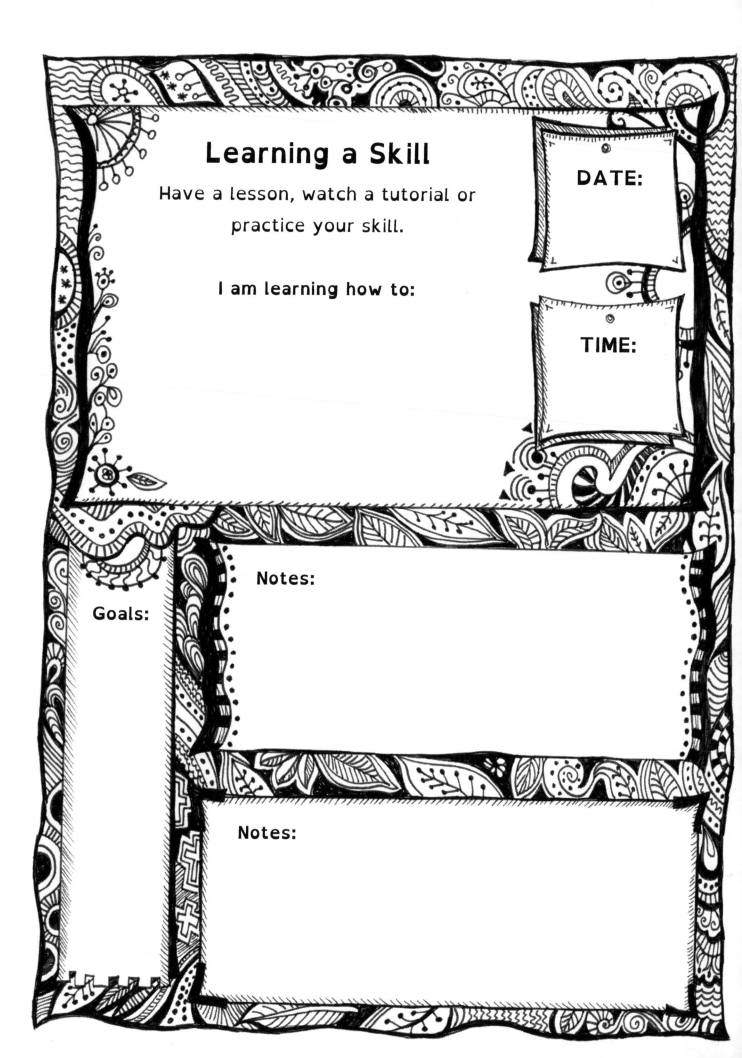

Learning a Skill

Have a lesson, watch a tutorial or practice your skill.

I am learning how to:

DATE:

TIME:

Goals:

Notes:

Notes:

Write & Draw
about something that really happened.

_____
_____
_____
_____
_____
_____
_____
_____
_____

Circle
Today's Date

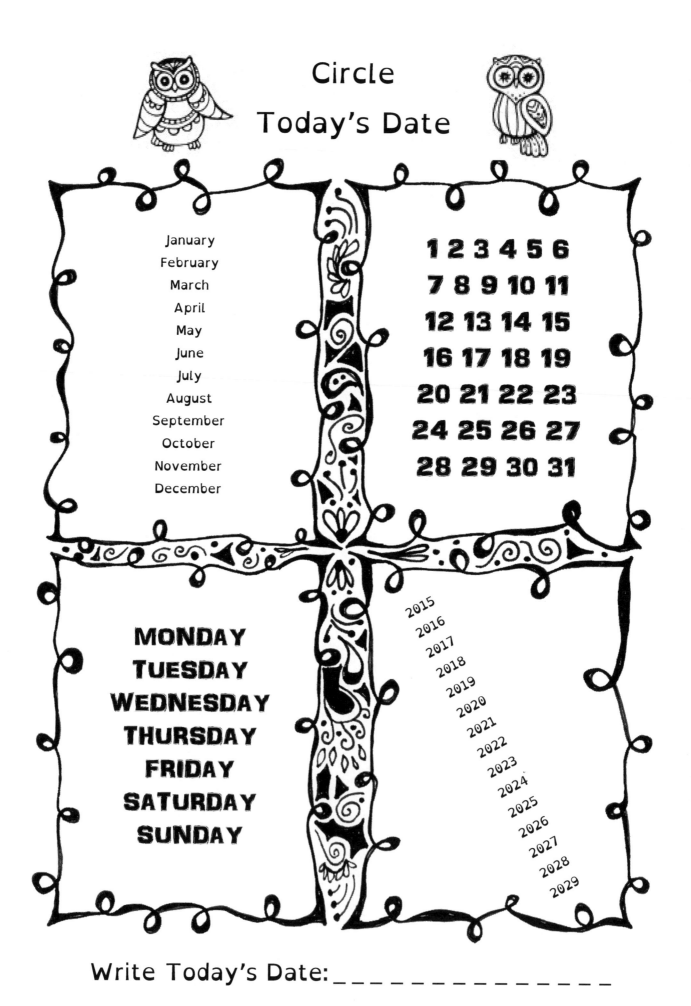

January
February
March
April
May
June
July
August
September
October
November
December

1 2 3 4 5 6
7 8 9 10 11
12 13 14 15
16 17 18 19
20 21 22 23
24 25 26 27
28 29 30 31

MONDAY
TUESDAY
WEDNESDAY
THURSDAY
FRIDAY
SATURDAY
SUNDAY

2015
2016
2017
2018
2019
2020
2021
2022
2023
2024
2025
2026
2027
2028
2029

Write Today's Date:_____

Nature Study

Go outside and make a realistic
drawing of something you find in nature.

Reading Time - 1 Hour

Choose Four Books - Read from each book for 15 minutes.

Copy a sentence or picture from each book here:

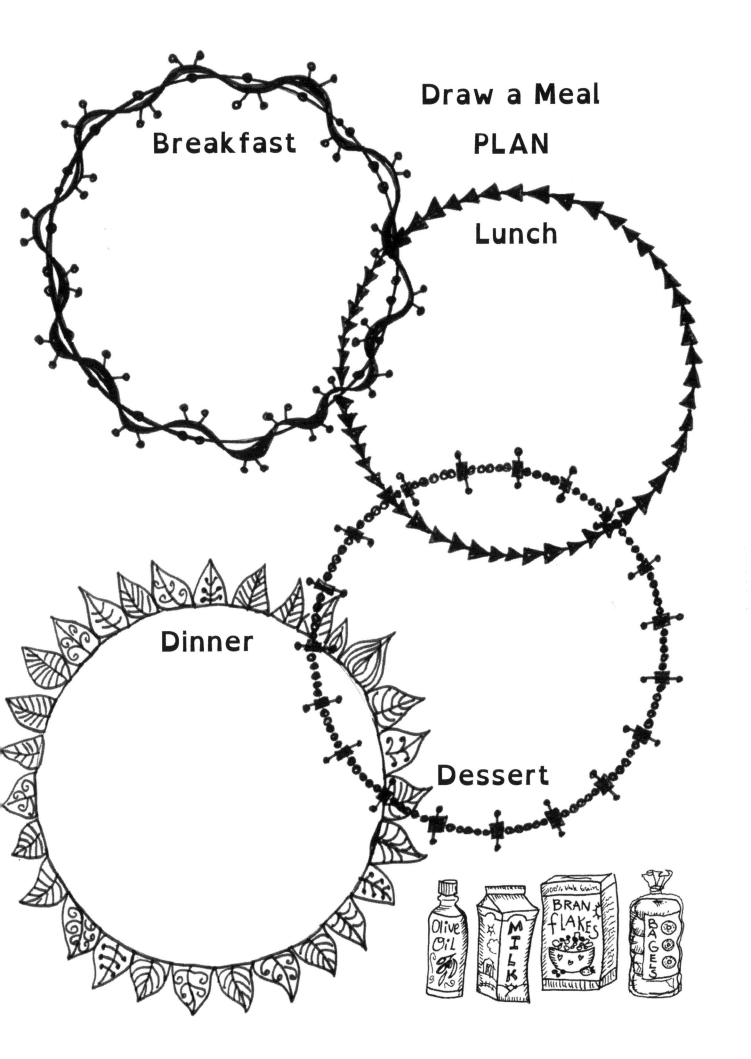

Breakfast

Draw a Meal
PLAN

Lunch

Dinner

Dessert

Circle Today's Date

January
February
March
April
May
June
July
August
September
October
November
December

1 2 3 4 5 6
7 8 9 10 11
12 13 14 15
16 17 18 19
20 21 22 23
24 25 26 27
28 29 30 31

MONDAY
TUESDAY
WEDNESDAY
THURSDAY
FRIDAY
SATURDAY
SUNDAY

2015
2016
2017
2018
2019
2020
2021
2022
2023
2024
2025
2026
2027
2028
2029

Write Today's Date: _ _ _ _ _ _ _ _ _ _ _ _ _ _ _ _ _

Spelling Time

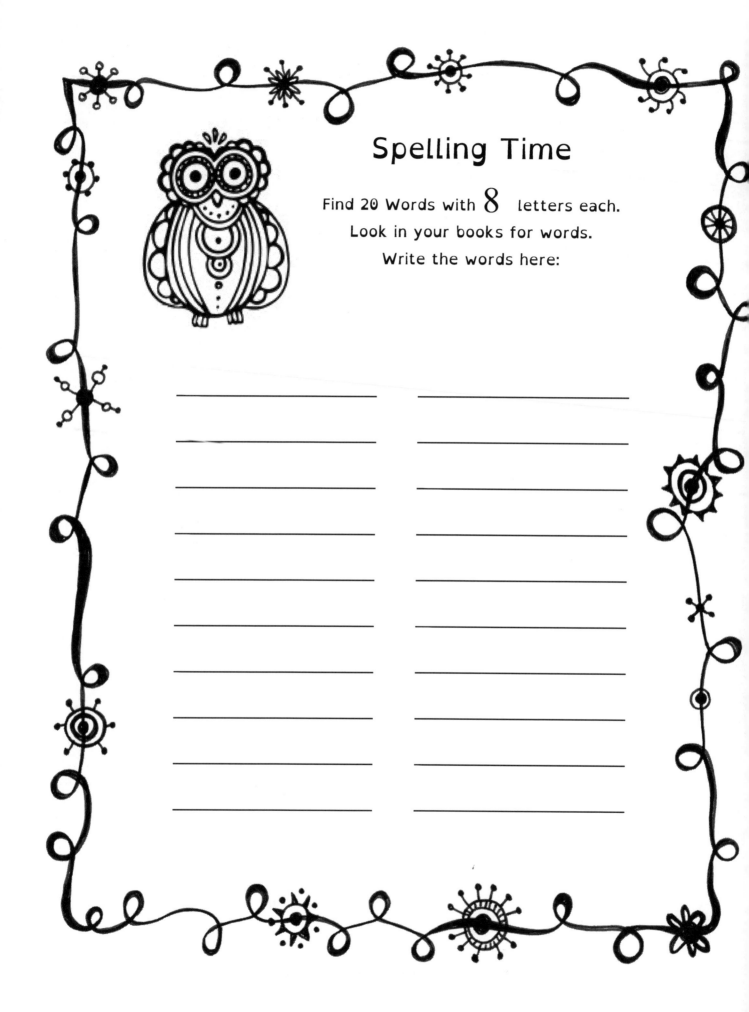

Find 20 Words with 8 letters each.

Look in your books for words.

Write the words here:

Film Study

Watch a Documentary, Educational Program or Movie

TITLE:

TIME:

TOPIC: _____

I learned:_____

_____

_____

_____

NOTES:

Draw a Scene From the Film:

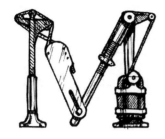

Math Practice

Watch a math tutorial or open up a math book.
You can practice math problems here.

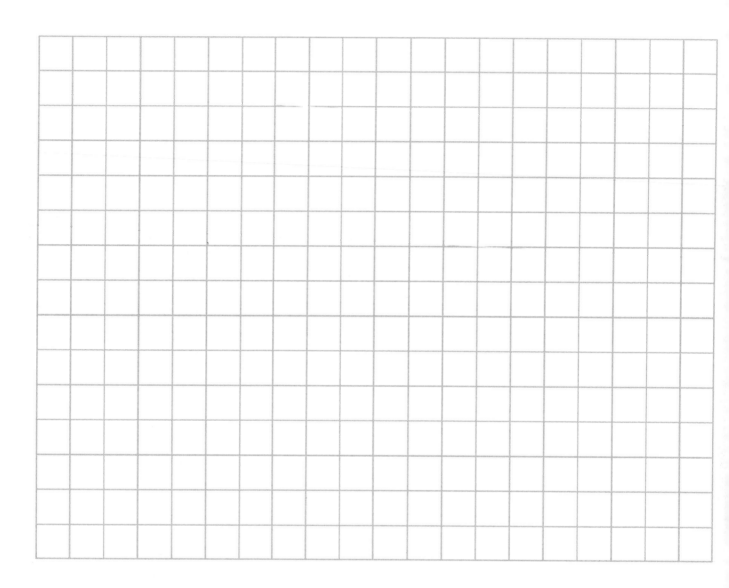

Copywork

Find an interesting paragraph in one of your books and copy it. Be diligent to make your writing look exactly like it does in the book.

TITLE:_____ **Page Number:_____**

_____

_____

_____

_____

_____

_____

_____

_____

_____

_____

_____

_____

_____

_____

_____

Sketch a Picture

Look through your library books and find something to draw.

Circle
Today's Date

January
February
March
April
May
June
July
August
September
October
November
December

1 2 3 4 5 6
7 8 9 10 11
12 13 14 15
16 17 18 19
20 21 22 23
24 25 26 27
28 29 30 31

MONDAY
TUESDAY
WEDNESDAY
THURSDAY
FRIDAY
SATURDAY
SUNDAY

2015
2016
2017
2018
2019
2020
2021
2022
2023
2024
2025
2026
2027
2028
2029

Write Today's Date: _ _ _ _ _ _ _ _ _ _ _ _ _ _ _

My Thinking Page

This is where you write down your ideas, goals, and plans - with a thankful heart!

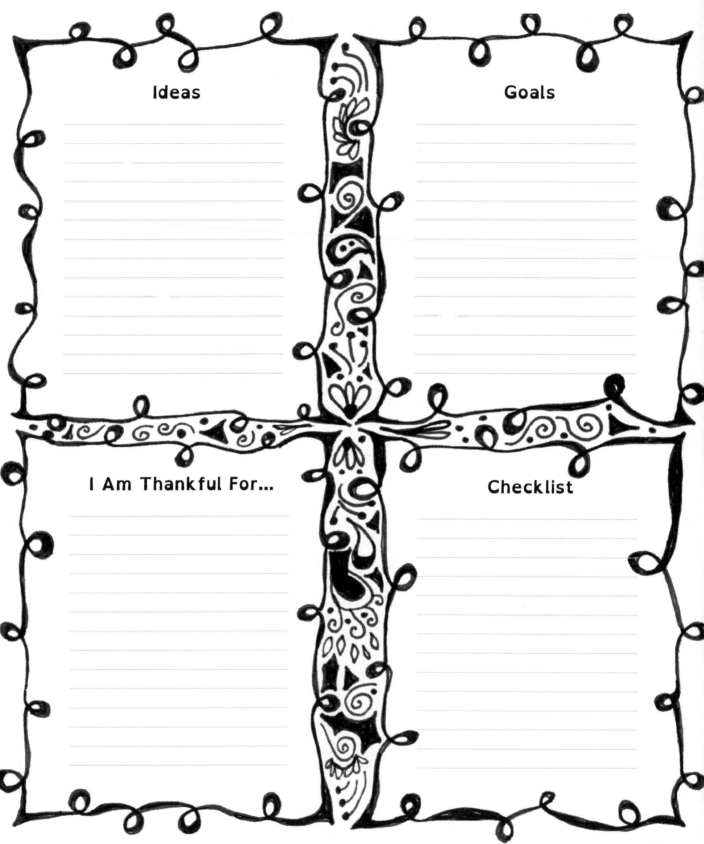

Ideas

Goals

I Am Thankful For...

Checklist

Write & Draw
about something that really happened.

_____

_____

_____

_____

_____

_____

_____

_____

_____

Nature Study

Go outside and make a realistic drawing of something you find in nature.

Reading Time - 1 Hour

Choose Four Books - Read from each book for 15 minutes.
Copy a sentence or picture from each book here:

Circle
Today's Date

January
February
March
April
May
June
July
August
September
October
November
December

1 2 3 4 5 6
7 8 9 10 11
12 13 14 15
16 17 18 19
20 21 22 23
24 25 26 27
28 29 30 31

MONDAY
TUESDAY
WEDNESDAY
THURSDAY
FRIDAY
SATURDAY
SUNDAY

2015
2016
2017
2018
2019
2020
2021
2022
2023
2024
2025
2026
2027
2028
2029

Write Today's Date: _ _ _ _ _ _ _ _ _ _ _ _ _ _ _ _

Film Study

Watch a Documentary, Educational Program or Movie

TITLE:

TIME:

TOPIC: _____

I learned: _____

_____

_____

_____

NOTES:

Draw a Scene From the Film:

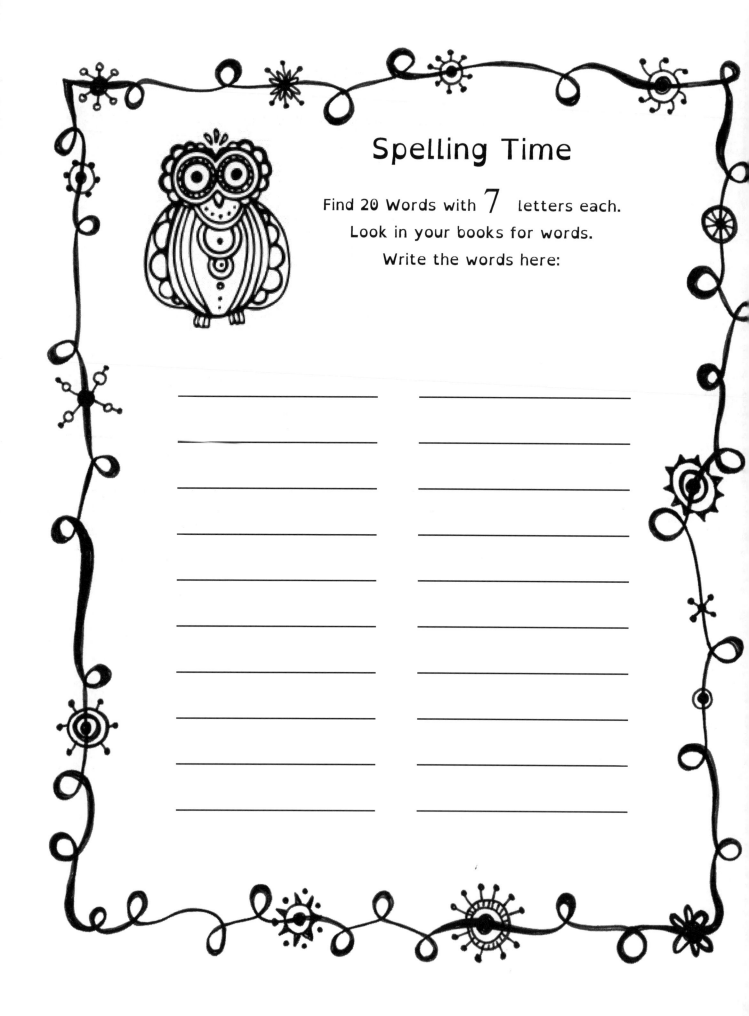

Spelling Time

Find 20 Words with 7 letters each.

Look in your books for words.

Write the words here:

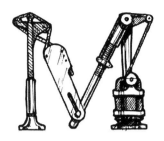

Math Practice

Watch a math tutorial or open up a math book.

You can practice math problems here.

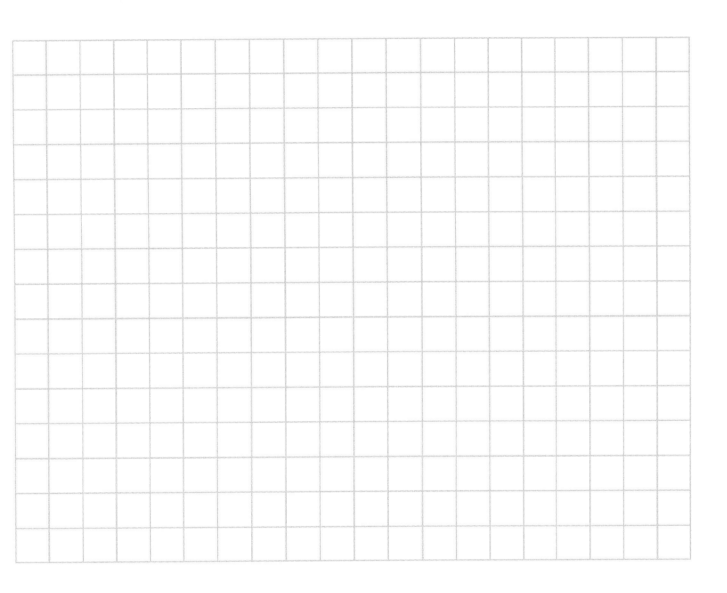

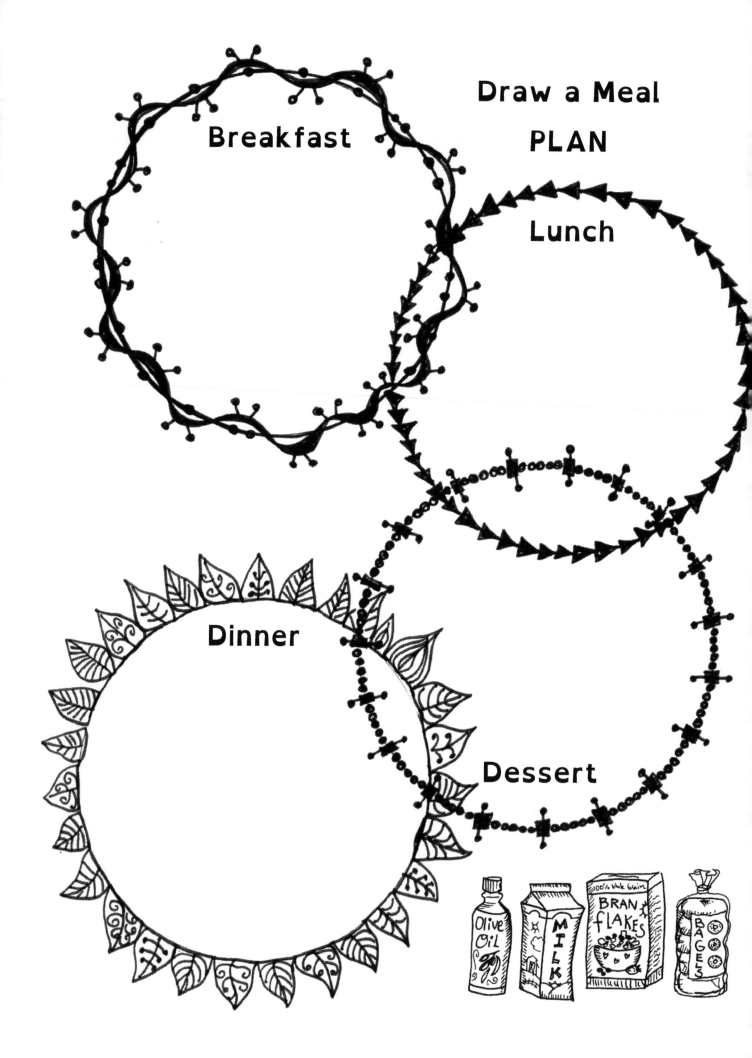

Breakfast

Draw a Meal
PLAN

Lunch

Dinner

Dessert

Copywork

Find an interesting paragraph in one of your books and copy it. Be diligent to make your writing look exactly like it does in the book.

TITLE:_____ **Page Number:**_____

_____

_____

_____

_____

_____

_____

_____

_____

_____

_____

_____

_____

_____

_____

_____

_____

Sketch a Picture

Look through your library books and find something to draw.

Circle
Today's Date

January
February
March
April
May
June
July
August
September
October
November
December

1 2 3 4 5 6
7 8 9 10 11
12 13 14 15
16 17 18 19
20 21 22 23
24 25 26 27
28 29 30 31

MONDAY
TUESDAY
WEDNESDAY
THURSDAY
FRIDAY
SATURDAY
SUNDAY

2015
2016
2017
2018
2019
2020
2021
2022
2023
2024
2025
2026
2027
2028
2029

Write Today's Date:_ _ _ _ _ _ _ _ _ _ _ _ _ _ _

My Thinking Page

This is where you write down your ideas, goals,
and plans - with a thankful heart!

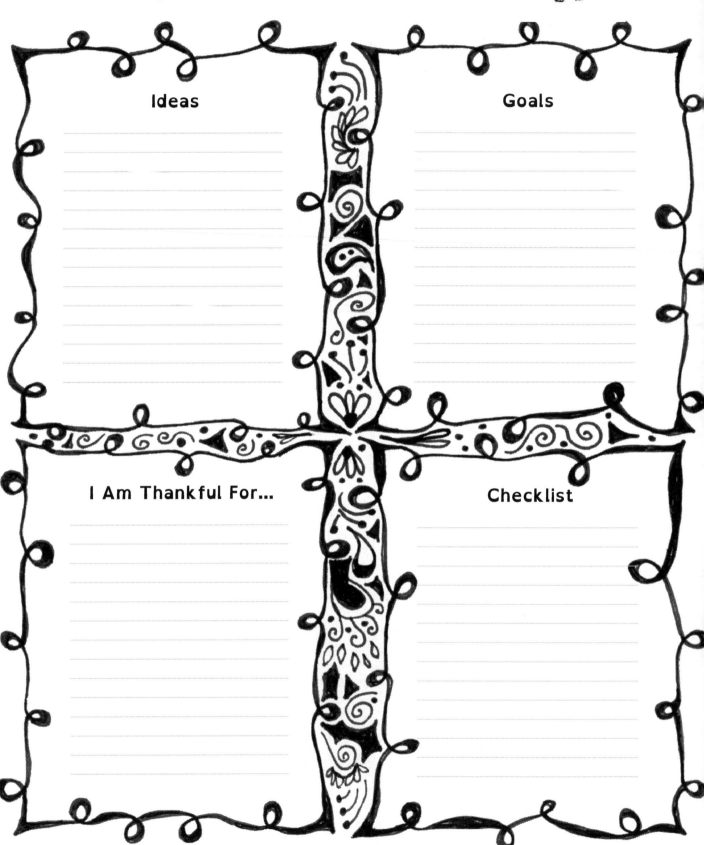

Ideas

Goals

I Am Thankful For...

Checklist

Nature Study

Go outside and make a realistic drawing of something you find in nature.

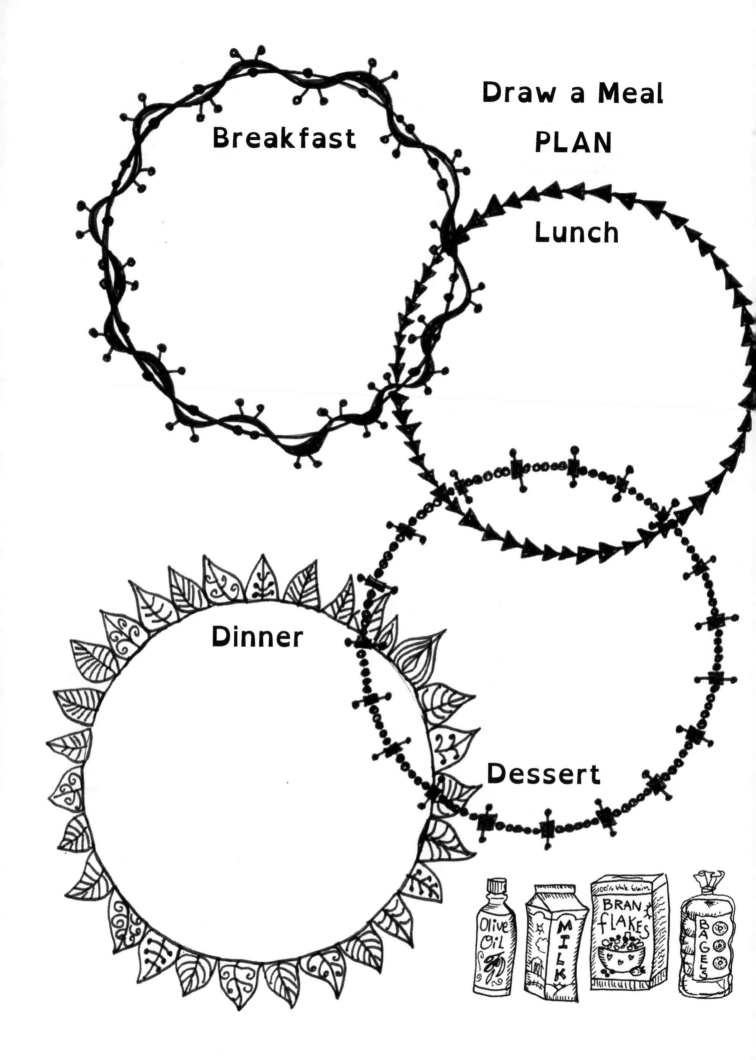

Reading Time - 1 Hour

Choose Four Books - Read from each book for 15 minutes.

Copy a sentence or picture from each book here:

Circle
Today's Date

January
February
March
April
May
June
July
August
September
October
November
December

1 2 3 4 5 6
7 8 9 10 11
12 13 14 15
16 17 18 19
20 21 22 23
24 25 26 27
28 29 30 31

MONDAY
TUESDAY
WEDNESDAY
THURSDAY
FRIDAY
SATURDAY
SUNDAY

2015
2016
2017
2018
2019
2020
2021
2022
2023
2024
2025
2026
2027
2028
2029

Write Today's Date: _____

Spelling Time

Find 20 Words with 7 letters each.

Look in your books for words.

Write the words here:

Film Study

Watch a Documentary, Educational Program or Movie

TITLE:

TIME:

TOPIC: _____

I learned:_____

_____

_____

_____

NOTES:

Draw a Scene From the Film:

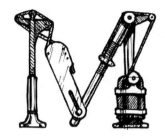

Math Practice

Watch a math tutorial or open up a math book.
You can practice math problems here.

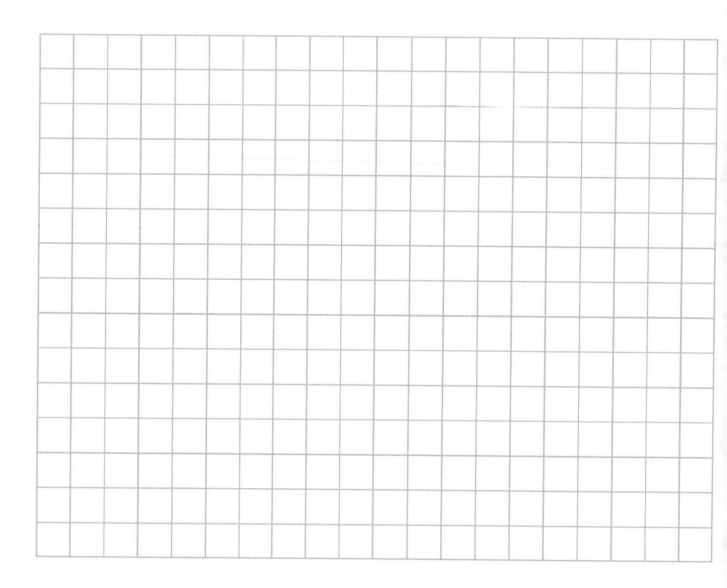

Copywork

Find an interesting paragraph in one of your books and copy it. Be diligent to make your writing look exactly like it does in the book.

TITLE:_____ **Page Number:**_____

_____

_____

_____

_____

_____

_____

_____

_____

_____

_____

_____

_____

_____

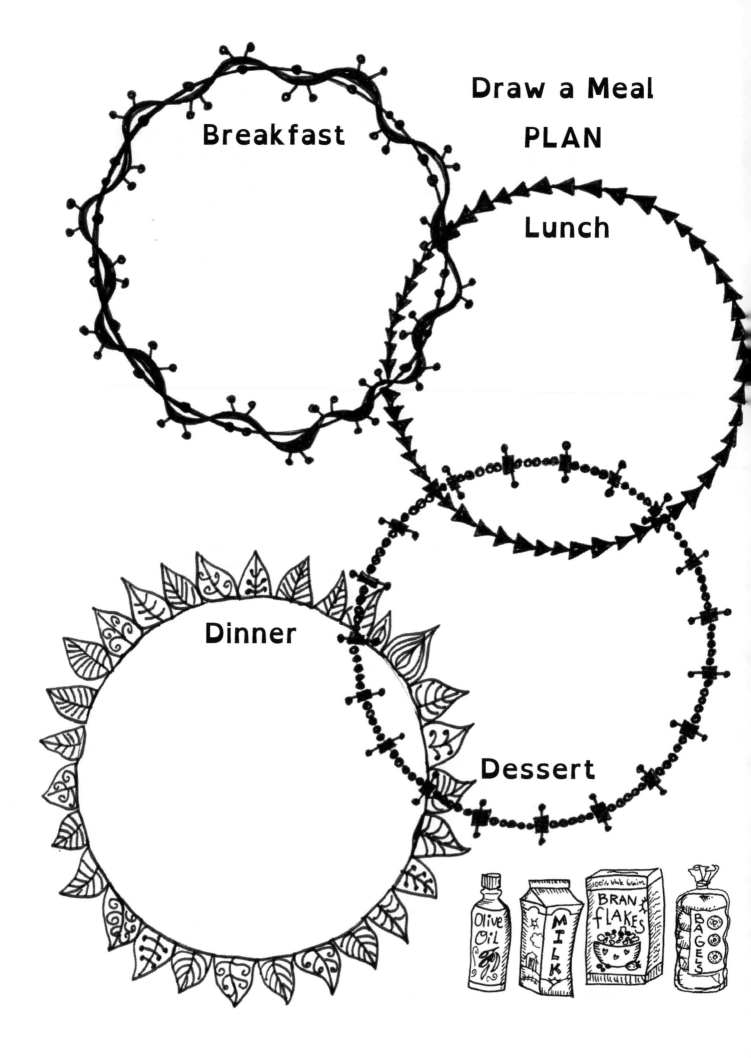

Breakfast

Draw a Meal
PLAN

Lunch

Dinner

Dessert

Circle Today's Date

January
February
March
April
May
June
July
August
September
October
November
December

1 2 3 4 5 6
7 8 9 10 11
12 13 14 15
16 17 18 19
20 21 22 23
24 25 26 27
28 29 30 31

MONDAY
TUESDAY
WEDNESDAY
THURSDAY
FRIDAY
SATURDAY
SUNDAY

2015
2016
2017
2018
2019
2020
2021
2022
2023
2024
2025
2026
2027
2028
2029

Write Today's Date:_ _ _ _ _ _ _ _ _ _ _ _ _ _ _ _

My Thinking Page

This is where you write down your ideas, goals, and plans - with a thankful heart!

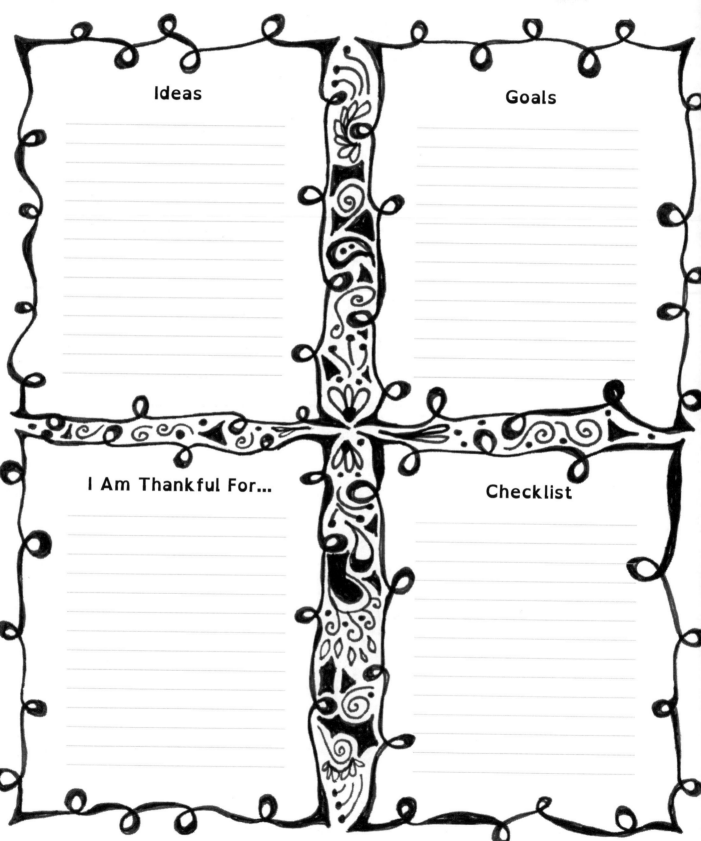

Ideas

Goals

I Am Thankful For...

Checklist

Write & Draw
about something that
really happened.

_____

_____

_____

_____

_____

_____

_____

_____

_____

_____

Nature Study

Go outside and make a realistic
drawing of something you find in nature.

Reading Time - 1 Hour

Choose Four Books - Read from each book for 15 minutes.

Copy a sentence or picture from each book here:

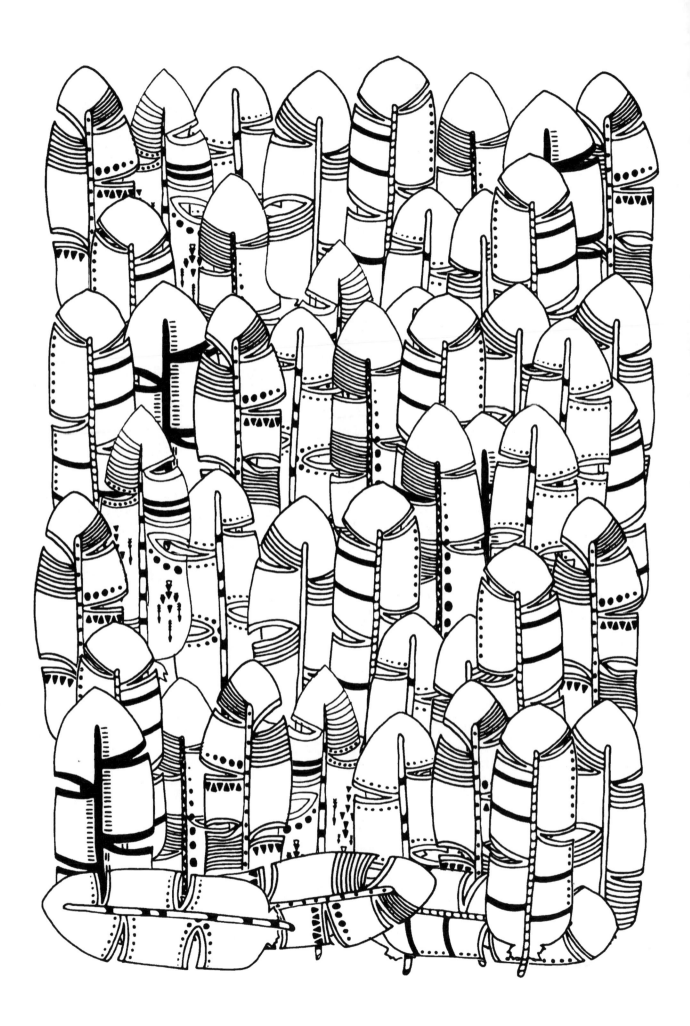

Circle
Today's Date

January
February
March
April
May
June
July
August
September
October
November
December

1 2 3 4 5 6
7 8 9 10 11
12 13 14 15
16 17 18 19
20 21 22 23
24 25 26 27
28 29 30 31

MONDAY
TUESDAY
WEDNESDAY
THURSDAY
FRIDAY
SATURDAY
SUNDAY

2015
2016
2017
2018
2019
2020
2021
2022
2023
2024
2025
2026
2027
2028
2029

Write Today's Date:_ _ _ _ _ _ _ _ _ _ _ _ _ _ _ _

Spelling Time

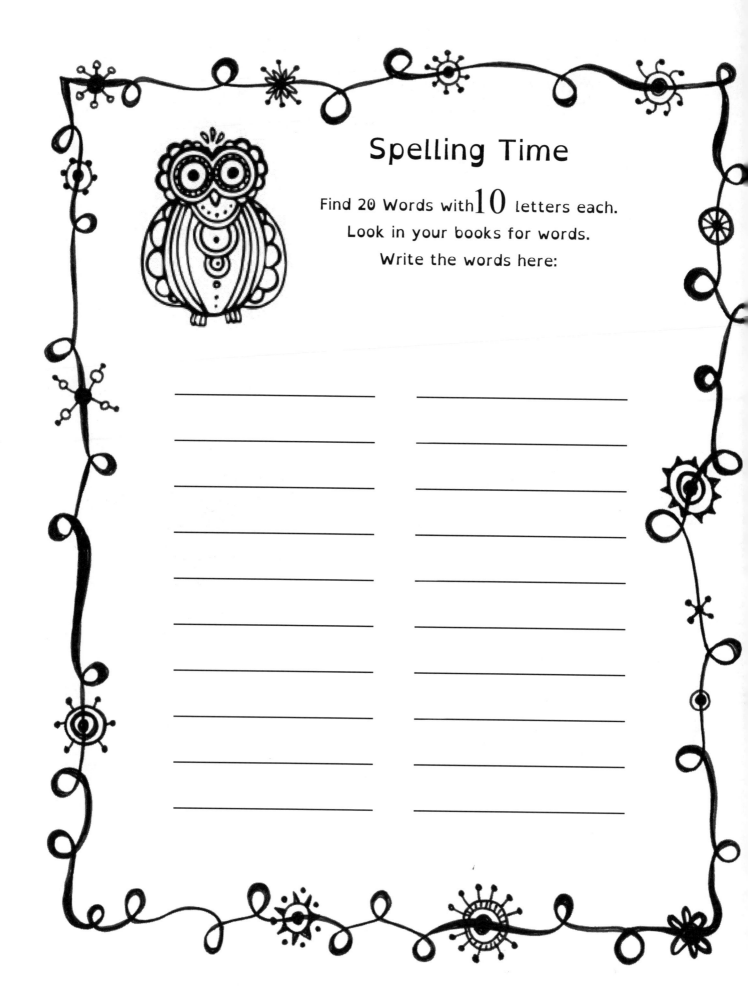

Find 20 Words with 10 letters each.
Look in your books for words.
Write the words here:

_____   _____

_____   _____

_____   _____

_____   _____

_____   _____

_____   _____

_____   _____

_____   _____

_____   _____

_____   _____

Film Study

Watch a Documentary, Educational Program or Movie

TIME:

TITLE:

TOPIC: _____

I learned: _____

_____

_____

_____

NOTES:

Draw a Scene From the Film:

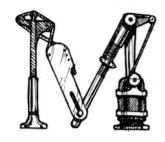

Math Practice

Watch a math tutorial or open up a math book.

You can practice math problems here.

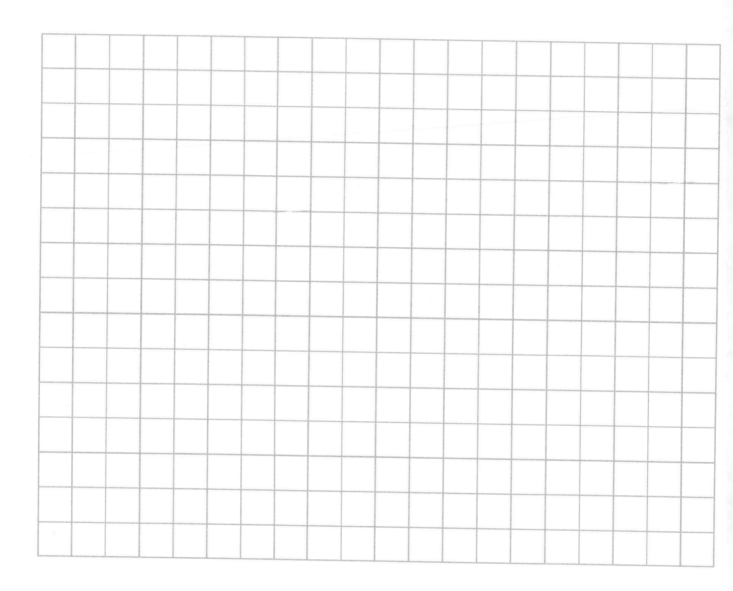

Copywork

Find an interesting paragraph in one of your books and copy it. Be diligent to make your writing look exactly like it does in the book.

TITLE:_____ **Page Number:_____**

_____

_____

_____

_____

_____

_____

_____

_____

_____

_____

_____

_____

_____

_____

_____

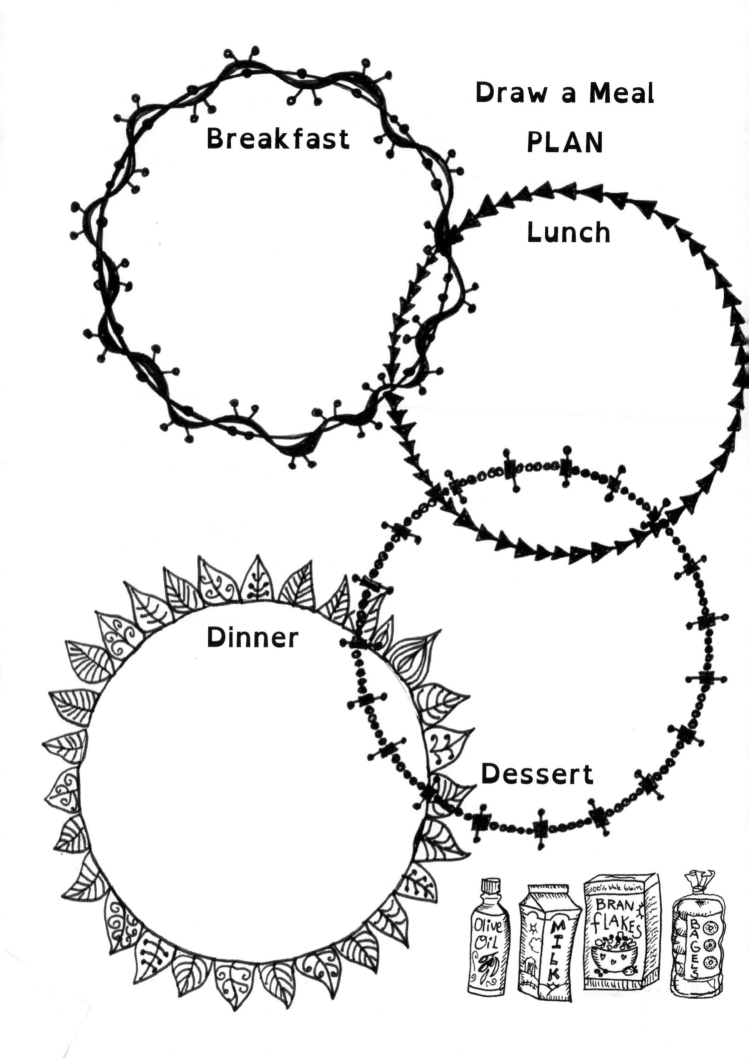

Draw a Meal PLAN

Breakfast

Lunch

Dinner

Dessert

Do It Yourself
HOMESCHOOL
JOURNALS

Copyright Information

Contact Us:

The Thinking Tree LLC

617 N. Swope St. Greenfield, IN 46140. United States

317.622.8852 PHONE (Dial +1 outside of the USA) 267.712.7889 FAX

www.DyslexiaGames.com

jbrown@DyslexiaGames.com

Made in the USA
San Bernardino, CA
04 December 2019